So.lu.tion.ary

[suh-**loo**-shuh-ner-ee]

noun

1. Disruptive innovator who creates transformational impact

2. Critical thinker who treats the root cause, not just the symptoms

3. Leader supporting a culture of innovation

4. Visionary who challenges conventional wisdom for a better way

Praise for *Solutionaries*

Linda Lattimore has inspired me and thousands of others over the years, and her book, *Solutionaries*, is designed to activate the compassion, love, energy and commitment to leave a legacy rather than liabilities. I encourage you to buy this book and work your way through it. You have it in you to make a greater contribution to the world and this book will help you figure out how.

Les Brown
Renowned motivational speaker
CEO/Founder, Les Brown Institute

So many today want to be part of the new solutions our world so desperately needs. We are not satisfied with naming the problems, we want answers and fresh ideas strong enough to impassion others to bring their best to the table and forge new paths together. Linda Lattimore, in her book *Solutionairies*, has created a map to guide and clarify, not only your deepest intentions, but also who you are so you can find your own Solutionary peers. This book crosses generational lines. It can be successfully used by the young and the old who are driven to make a difference. This book should be on the shelf of every job recruiter, psychologist, school counselor and in every household with anyone about to embark into the world for the first time or the twentieth time.

Rosa Glenn Reilly
Director and Founder, Spectrum Center, Houston

Given the current issues and challenges facing humanity today, Linda Lattimore reminds each of us that there is hope for a more loving and kinder world when we each accept the challenge to do our part. Insightful and thought-provoking, *Solutionaries* provides a step-by-step guide that reveals the gifts and talents each of us has to offer and then provides a destination for them—allowing us to live more relevant and meaningful lives.

Lynne Twist
Author of *Soul of Money*
Co-Founder, Pachamama Alliance

All of us wish that we could fix situations that are broken, but often we don't know where to begin. *Solutionaries* is a beacon of light that illuminates your path, enabling you to find work to live a life of happiness and purpose. Through my battle with breast cancer, I discovered the Solutionary in me. After the shocking discovery of the lack of post-mastectomy equipment to recover in, I designed and patented the healincomfort® recovery shirt. Learn how you can discover the Solutionary in you by using this workbook!

Cherie B. Matthews
Founder and CEO, healincomfort

Linda Lattimore's insightful book, *Solutionaries*, is a much-needed breath of fresh air during a time when so many are searching for more meaning and fulfillment in their lives. Her method artfully ushers you through a process of self-discovery that shines a light on the untapped gifts and talents you are here to share with the world. No matter where you are in life or what kind of work you already do, *Solutionaries* is the perfect companion on your journey to more happiness, joy and contribution.

Jane Deuber
CEO, Global Experts Accelerator

Working with students eager to make a difference and be the change they want to see in this world often reveals the lack of literature specifically dedicated to offer a systematic approach to this common desire. Linda Lattimore's *Solutionaries* fills this void and reminds us, with a familiar and approachable tone, that living a happier more meaningful life is actually possible, regardless of our profession, skills or area of expertise.

Rogelio Garcia Contreras
Director of Social Innovation, University of Arkansas

As someone who works with later-stage professionals in reinventing their careers, Lattimore's methodology is a welcome toolset for those seeking to turn their careers around, recover from the malaise that often hits at this point in life, and set themselves on a solid course for success in their second act. It is an empowering methodology that will program you for success in this next phase of your career.

John Tarnoff
Reinvention career coach and speaker
Author of *Boomer Reinvention*

SOLUTIONARIES:
You Are the Answer!

By Linda Lattimore

EMERALD LAKE
BOOKS

To Rachel and Allie,
my reasons for being,

and

To Tegan,
my daily dose of inspiration.

Contents

Step Six **135**

Each Step You Take

Worksheets

Do not be dismayed by the brokenness of the world.
All things break. And all things can be mended.
Not with time, as they say, but with intention.
So go. Love intentionally, extravagantly, unconditionally.
The broken world waits in darkness for the light that is you.

— L. R. Knost

Foreword

I believe you need to be hungry for the pathway to your greatness, to your dream and your destiny. By that, I mean you have to be hungry enough to make what you desire happen, no matter what.

When you have goals and dreams, there will be some resistance. An airplane cannot fly without the resistance of air. You can't learn good horsemanship by riding a tame horse. And the harder the battle, the sweeter the victory.

Sometimes that resistance comes from within us, speared on by uncertainty. Other times, it comes from the outside, prompted by others' opinions or financial limitations.

Yet for many people, as they look around at the world today, they see all that's wrong with it and wonder why someone doesn't do something about it. They often miss seeing that they are the ones who can make things better if only they were willing to apply their gifts and talents to the causes and issues they're passionate about. They are the missing piece to the puzzle!

Since you've picked up this book, *Solutionaries*, by my friend, Linda Lattimore, my guess is, that doesn't describe you. You want to get off the bench line of life, to step into life. You want to be a part of the solution, not a part of the problem.

If that sounds like you, then you've chosen the right book and the right teacher to guide you through the process so you can discover how you fit into the solution.

Linda is a leader, a visionary, and a disruptor. And she's proud of it! More than that, though, she believes we're all here to serve each other. In her thoughts in this area, there is something that we can all identify with and embrace.

My favorite book says, "The greatest among you will be your servant." I encourage you to embrace your greatness and disarm the resistance you may encounter. You have it in you to make a greater contribution to life. So don't play small.

You have something special. You have greatness in you. That's my story and I'm sticking to it.

Les Brown
Renowned motivational speaker
CEO/Founder, Les Brown Institute

Prologue

I was conceived in Manila, Philippines, at Clark AFB, and was born in Fort Worth, Texas, the daughter of a very young couple navigating the challenges of military life at the end of WWII. Upon their return to Texas, my father took a sales position with a pharmaceutical company and my mother worked hard to be a proper housewife, devoting her days to raising her daughters and helping her husband scale the corporate ladder. By the time I was five, we had moved to Lima, Peru, followed by Mexico City DF, as he entered the international world of business.

Following along on each step of his journey, I learned to appreciate the history and antiquities of the places we lived while becoming fluent in other languages. The most important lesson of all was, I learned to know no strangers. Race, religion or socioeconomic circumstances posed no barrier. Even at a young age, it was clear to me there were those who had much, but more who had little. I witnessed extreme poverty in several developing countries during my formative years, often finding myself face-to-face with other small children who were hungry, holding their palms up to me, no parents in sight.

As I began to think of college, my hope was to become a social worker, to help those on the outskirts, but my father wanted to ensure I could take care of myself financially, so he steered me to finance and legal degrees.

Many years later, after my children had left the nest, I found myself in the world of microfinance through a series of unexpected and seemingly random circumstances. As a result, I founded Women's Global Network, a women's business networking organization, and the WGN Global Fund, a 501(c)(3), whose mission is to support and educate women about social enterprise as a vehicle for change. WGN grew into a large membership network of professional women in the US and abroad who felt a responsibility to help women less fortunate around the world with small loans.

The power of the collective was humbling and inspiring. Hundreds of disadvantaged women were funded and children who had previously been unable to go to school received money for uniforms and transportation. Their lives were improving and our members appreciated their own good fortune even more after travelling to Africa and Latin America to meet their global business partners.

As for me, it felt as though I was engaging with the very mothers of the small children I had been face-to-face with as a five-year old. Only this time, I had a lifetime of experiences and a wealth of knowledge, and I could help.

I had a business degree and a law degree. As a corporate executive, I knew what it took to start a business. I could speak other languages and felt a kinship to their cultures. I had been a single mother with two young daughters under the age of five and remembered what it felt like to lay awake at night not knowing where the money would come from or how I would manage through the challenges ahead of me. I could relate to these women and offer them encouragement and business tools—the value I could provide them was tangible. The difference between my dreams and desires of helping at 16 and 50 was the life experience I had gained along my journey.

I am clear now that each of us has an important role, a unique piece to the jigsaw puzzle of life, that cannot be completed without our gifts and talents, the most important of which are not always learned through formal education or work experience. My life has been a constant quest to equalize the playing field, to find solutions, and to make a difference.

After being contacted by a number of people wanting to help, but unclear how to, I began to understand how deep this hunger runs in many of us and how pervasive it is in our communities. Fundamentally, our desire is to be of service and to have a positive impact on others.

While digital overload screams urgency in our faces every day—about climate-related catastrophes, political chaos and discord, human rights issues from trafficking to pay equalization, fear and unrest on the streets, in our offices and schools—it's hard on many days to feel a sense of joy, much less purpose. It's even harder to understand how we can help when the issues seem insurmountable. We are just ordinary people navigating our own daily hurdles. So, we are left much like a deer in the headlights, paralyzed, not moving forward or backward, as the problems we witness get closer to our own backyards.

It takes a village, a community, friends and advocates. It takes "Solutionaries"—those who see a problem and are willing to step up and try to fix it. Each of us has walked a different life path, giving us unique talents and skills no one else on the planet has. There are issues that touch us and call to us because of those experiences.

Unfortunately, numerous books tell us we must have a "purpose" or "passion," but figuring out what that is can be daunting for many. These words have become overused buzz words, leaving many people feeling inadequate because they can't identify with or connect to concepts so encompassing. The words are limiting as they attempt to bind each of us to a single purpose when, in actuality, we have many, and they will evolve as we grow and continue to gain wisdom and additional talents on our journey.

It took me many years and a lot of reflection to understand why social enterprise was so important to me. It started when I was five but did not manifest until my fifties. And then, looking back, it all made sense.

This book is a study of your life journey to help you get clarity on your piece of the puzzle. Often the benefit of hindsight is overshadowed by our constant peering into the future, but it is our greatest teacher and sets the foundation for all that is to come.

I'm excited to walk this path with you and look forward to meeting you in the world of innovation. Remember, you hold unique answers and we need your wisdom. Our puzzle is not complete without you.

Before We Get Started

How to Use This Book

In this workbook, we will go through a step-by-step process to help you identify the values you bring to the world based on your own experiences and how they align with the causes that need you the most.

The work will be enlightening, inspirational and life-changing as you:

- Discover the talents, gifts and tools that make you uniquely qualified to lead.

- Present your distinct value proposition (Brand You) to the world with intention.

- Identify compelling issues that drive you to serve and make a difference.

- Find and join your tribe of like-minded "Solutionaries" and changemakers.

- Create an action plan for a life that meets both your financial and emotional needs.

This journey consists of six steps, and I have provided three lessons for each step as well as related exercises to help you work through this process of self-discovery. It is important that you don't skip a step or complete the exercises out of order since each one builds upon the knowledge you gained in the previous one, not unlike life itself.

Feel free to fill out the exercises in the book or to keep a separate journal, but I urge you to take the time to answer the questions and reflect on them as you go through this process.

As always, at the end of any exercise, be sure to go back to fill in any blanks and check your answers to make sure you are happy with them. This book will ask thought-provoking questions of you, requiring the most honest answers you can give at the time. As you continue to reflect, you may want to adjust earlier answers—and that's fine! Frankly, to remain authentic and current, it's a good idea to review your answers regularly. Your life and experiences are a moving force and may necessitate updating what you have written.

Additional Resources

As you read through this book, each lesson has exercises for you to complete. Some lessons reference additional resources, or templates, to be used. All templates are available at solutionariesacademy.com/templates.

There are also bonus materials available to you as well. These offer a variety of lists and ideas to help you as you think about your own responses to the questions asked in the book. These can be found at solutionariesacademy.com/bonuses.

If at any point in time you feel like you're getting stuck and would enjoy my personal encouragement and a community of kindred spirits as you navigate through the exercises in this book, check out my small group masterminds at solutionariesacademy.com/illuminate.

Guided Meditation

We have all heard about the benefits of meditation, which include stress reduction, improved health, more restful sleep, slowed aging, emotional stability, positive thinking, happiness and improved quality of life. I confess I'm not always consistent with a daily practice when time is short and work and family demands call. But I have found meditation to be especially helpful in finding clarity when I am puzzling through a dilemma or making a big decision. In those times, if I can just stop thinking, stewing and striving to find the answer and step away for a little while, the solution will generally present itself.

As you work with this book, you are going to be digging deep on your quest for a new way of living that gives you a greater sense of purpose and satisfaction. Before you can look to the future, it is helpful to identify the lessons you have learned throughout your life that have influenced who you are today.

To get your creative juices flowing, let's call on your subconscious to lend you a hand with a guided meditation. This process will take you on a walk down "memory lane," recalling influential people and impactful experiences through mental imagery. It should be fun and give you a sense of peace and ease as you get ready to take the plunge. You can either read the following guided meditation, record your own voice and then play it back as you do the exercise, or listen to the audio we have provided in our materials online. You can find it at solutionariesacademy.com/meditation.

Take a moment to make sure you are seated comfortably. Rest your hands loosely in your lap. Now, close your eyes.

Take a long… slow… deep breath in. Hold it to a gradual count of ten and then leisurely exhale through your mouth, completely emptying your lungs.

Do this exercise three more times… holding the breath

on the inhale for ten seconds... and pausing after the exhale for ten seconds... before you start again.

Continue to breathe slowly and gently as you bring your awareness to the very top of your head.

Imagine a warm comforting flow that starts at the crown and begins to move down your neck... spreading across your shoulders and down your arms... past your elbows to the palms of your hands... through your fingers to their very tips.

This gentle flow moves down your back and your chest... warming the small of your back and your core... circling your hips and thighs... it travels downward to your knees, calves and feet... filling the spaces between all your toes... and spilling onto the ground beneath your feet.

It is absorbed by the earth and tethers you closely, but lovingly, to the firmness of the ground. You feel safe and secure and centered... with no thoughts of anything... but this warm... nurturing energy.

After a few minutes, your mind wanders. Something catches your attention. You look up and you find yourself in a wooded area. In the distance, you see a sunlit, crystalline lake through the trees and you begin to walk down a path toward the translucent, sparkling water.

The air is cool and misty. You can smell the moisture in the air and feel the dampness on your skin. There are wood ferns and moss hanging from the trees with small, tiny purple violets and white orchids tucked between the rocks.

Focused on reaching the water's edge, you step into a clearing and follow a well-worn path down to the lake. You notice the path continues in a large circle around the lake, meandering around rocks and tall plants.

As you begin walking down the path, there are landmarks you recognize, worn but familiar, with most in the same order they had come into your life. You realize the path around this beautiful lake is your life path and, as you continue taking steps forward, you begin to see people who have crossed your path before. Take a closer look at the crowd of people.

Who do you see that you have loved? Do you see your first love? Your last? Do you see family members? Your parents? Your children? Other extended family? Dear friends? You are not in a rush. You want to honor those who have cared about you and offered you support, and to say "thank you" to them.

Do you see people who have hurt you? Did you learn anything from the experiences presented to you? Are you better for it or do you still carry the anger and hurt? Can you reflect with honesty and be thankful for the lessons you have learned?

You continue to walk slowly down the path, feeling the cool breeze on your face as it ruffles your hair... taking another long slow breath.

Your first job has appeared in front of you. Do you remember how green you were? Perhaps a little awkward and young? This was followed by other jobs. Were they more challenging or frustrating? Who do you see that you still think of fondly as a great example or mentor, someone who showed you the ropes and encouraged you? Were there many?

If you see moments when you were discouraged with those who were poor teachers or poor leaders in your workplace, who were they and how do you believe they failed? Did you learn to be a better example for those who walked behind you?

As you slowly walk, you think about people you never met but who you admired from afar and looked up to. Who were they and what was it about those people that you admired? What special traits did they have that no one else seemed to have? Were there others in the public eye who you wanted to distance yourself from? Why?

You keep walking, focused on the path, trying to avoid stumbling. You have almost made your way around the lake and suddenly the trail is unmarked. The plants are growing across it, unruly and unkempt, and you look behind you uncertain what you should do. The folks standing behind you are waving and urging you on and you take another deep breath as you get ready... ready for the next unknown adventure with the comfort that you have learned so much from those behind you, standing there supporting you... knowing as you clear the path and move forward, you can always rely on the wisdom you have gained each step of this journey.

As you get ready to come back to the present moment, keep the image of your authentic self with you, the one who forged the path to become the person you are today. Acknowledge all of the people and experiences that have been part of your life's journey, honoring each and every lesson learned.

It's time to come back now and get some work done…

Wiggle your fingers, waking up your hands and arms…

Move your toes, allowing your feet and legs to wake up…

Stretch and move your head from side to side…

Take a deep slow breath and…

Open your eyes and sit quietly for a moment while you reorient to your surroundings.

Step One

Discovering Natural Aptitude...
Your "Other DNA"

*Solutionaries have a broad,
360° view of their lives
and the world around them.*

Discover Your Natural Aptitude

You have joined the ranks of many like-minded people who yearn to make a difference, perhaps even leave a legacy of some sort. As someone who would like to make a positive impact on the world, you are uniquely qualified to lead the charge or participate with other kindred spirits in your quest to create change or fix a pressing issue. No one else on the planet has the distinctive skill set that is "Company You." To understand your unique value proposition, it's important you sit down and carefully decode and define your "other" DNA. I call this "Discovering Natural Aptitude"—quantifying the sum of your experiences and choices up to this point in time.

DNA is that one-of-a-kind imprint each of us is born with that makes us unlike any other human being on the planet. It's a marker and an identifier we had nothing to do with, yet our traits and characteristics are attributed to this unseen stamp. Your persona, however, has another type of DNA born from individual experiences and encounters with others that have left lasting effects on the way you lead your life and navigate the business world. You may be acutely aware of their impact or they may be tucked away in your subconscious, but either way they contribute to who you are and how you respond to people and situations.

Often, we default to a litany of skills we have acquired through education or job experience without fully understanding the wisdom we have acquired through life experiences. Yet these life experiences frequently result in the very values that act as our guideposts and boundaries. They reflect the things that mean the most to us. With knowledge comes an authenticity and a clear understanding of your value proposition so you will be able to expertly articulate it to your team, your customers, a potential employer, or as an advocate for a cause. Most importantly, it allows you to concisely and confidently respond to the question everyone needs an answer to, "Why you?"

In Lesson One of this step, you will examine the baseline from which you operate today, the descriptors you use to describe your skills and talents to others, and the work experiences you have historically been attracted to.

In Lesson Two, you will begin to create your autobiography by looking at the life experiences that have made you unique and special. Often these experiences give us the values with which we operate in our everyday encounters.

And finally, in Lesson Three, you will begin to visualize the journey ahead, one where you will connect the dots to find work that brings you both financial rewards and emotional fulfillment.

Lesson One:
Labels and Limitations

Before you start the process of looking at how life experiences have formed your values and the more intrinsic characteristics you use as a leader, let's look at the skills and talents you verbally default to on bios, resumes, job interviews or proposals. Often, when we think of our skills and talents, we think of them in terms of our professional skill set. After all, sailors learn how to sail, drivers learn how to drive, and pilots learn how to fly. Our automatic "go to" on resumes, bios and sales presentations are often words that illustrate our formal education, management experience, financial know-how or our impact to the company's bottom line.

Take a moment to answer the questions below as a starting point for the work you will do ahead. Keep in mind, this is not where you want to go or how you want to be, but who you currently are.

1. List five to ten words you use to describe yourself on your resume, bio or online profile to show you are qualified to pilot a particular project, get a job or run a committee.

    _____
    _____
    _____
    _____
    _____

2. Did you obtain your skills through formal or informal education? Please describe.

_____

_____

_____

_____

_____

_____

_____

3. In the past, what have you listed as your objective on your resume, online profiles or other sales and marketing materials? Has this changed? Describe.

_____

_____

_____

_____

_____

_____

_____

_____

4. What job descriptions have you historically been attracted to? Has this changed? Be detailed.

_____

_____

_____

_____

_____

_____

_____

_____

14

5. Has your focus been on the pay, the job description, emotional fulfillment or something else? Has this changed? Describe.

    _____

    _____

    _____

    _____

    _____

    _____

    _____

    _____

6. Are your skills and talents a result of hard work in the corporate world or the challenge of entrepreneurship? Describe.

    _____

    _____

    _____

    _____

    _____

    _____

    _____

    _____

7. How have you connected with those you serve through work or volunteering? Are you happier working remotely or in a more social setting? Do you text or email? Prefer to call or meet in person?

    _____

    _____

    _____

    _____

    _____

    _____

    _____

8. Have you faced the very issues your customers, clients or nonprofit constituents face? How do you relate to them? Be specific.

_____

_____

_____

_____

_____

_____

_____

_____

9. What titles or labels do you use for yourself and what do you hope they reflect?

_____

_____

_____

_____

_____

_____

_____

_____

When you look back at how you have searched for fulfilling work previously, you may have gone about it much the same way each time you transferred jobs. In many instances, the outcomes may not have been all that different with each new position. The tasks or pay might have varied, but the emotional fulfillment piece still left something to be desired.

Are you ready to try something new? It's amazing what reflection followed by thoughtful and subtle shifts can do. Let's keep moving forward.

Lesson Two:
A Look at the Road Behind You

Did you ever play Candyland as a child? It might have been the first game I learned to play. It required no reading and minimal counting skills, just a knowledge of colors, a love of sweets, and a desire to compete. It taught me that sometimes you get stuck in places like Molasses Swamp or Lollipop Woods, or you encounter "cherry pitfalls" and might have to wait patiently to cross over Gumdrop Mountain or wander through Peppermint Forest. But if you kept at it, kept trying to be the best, you could be the first to reach Candy Castle. The patience and motivation such games teach are values I've carried with me since childhood.

As a grown-up and someone who is all about business that has a community giveback, what makes the game equally special for me is its history. The game was created in 1948 by a teacher named Eleanor Abbott while she was recovering from polio in San Diego, California. This was during one of the more severe outbreaks of the polio epidemic in the U.S. and Eleanor wanted to create a simple game to cheer up children recovering from the disease. It was made for and tested by children in the same wards at the hospital she was recuperating in. The game went on to make millions for Milton Bradley and its successors, but a social purpose was its genesis.

That's my idea of a win: The resolution of a socially pressing issue to the benefit and profit of others.

Having the vantage of hindsight now, I see all of my experiences have either been the genesis of a new idea or the refinement of an aptitude or talent. And I continue to add new ones each day. Experiences mold our values, whereas repetition and education are what help us refine a skill set. Understanding why certain values are important to us allows us to explain to others with authenticity what we are all about and why.

Your brain subconsciously captures everything you see, hear or experience throughout your life. It then stores everything as a memory, even the filters, such as desires and dreams or fears and frustrations. Who you are and how you see yourself is the result of everything your brain has catalogued.

In this next section, you will take a look at your autobiography. The exercise below will ask you to write about certain situations or people who left an impact on you. You may remember them as joyful or painful but it is likely that through them you learned some type of valuable life lesson. Our experiences leave an imprint on us and our stories help explain the things that are important to us and how we navigate life.

After you answer the questions that follow, try to distill each one you record into one word that captures what you learned in the situation or from a particular person. Here is the important part: the word you write must be positive. For example, rather than saying, "I learned never to trust again," you might reframe this thought and write, "I learned to be *discerning*" using the word "discerning" as your key word from the experience.

How you frame your experience is critical to appreciating what you learned and how the experience provided you with the guideposts and boundaries within which you operate today. If you are having trouble with reframing words so they have a positive impact, I have created a guide to help you, *Prism – Reflections of You*, which you can download at solutionariesacademy.com/bonuses. So, let's get started!

1. **Welcome to the World!** Describe the family you were born into, the circumstances of your birth and how they affected you.

   _____

   _____

   _____

   _____

   _____

   _____

   _____

   _____

   _____

   Your word: _____

2. **Your Childhood Years**: Describe a situation from your childhood that shifted your perception of the world.

   _____

   _____

   _____

   _____

   _____

   _____

   _____

   _____

   _____

   Your word: _____

3. **The Tumultuous Teens**: Describe someone who taught you an important lesson and what you learned.

_____
_____
_____
_____
_____
_____
_____
_____
_____

Your word: _____

4. **First Time Away**: Tell a funny story about something that happened to you when you first moved away from home and how it changed your point of view.

_____
_____
_____
_____
_____
_____
_____
_____
_____

Your word: _____

5. **Best Friend:** Describe the best friend you've ever had, what you value the most about them and what makes them special.

_____
_____
_____
_____

_____

_____

_____

_____

_____

Your word: _____

6. **Working 9–5**: Talk about a situation at a job, good or bad, that left a lasting impression on the way you conduct business or with whom.

_____

_____

_____

_____

_____

_____

_____

_____

Your word: _____

7. **Travel**: Describe a special trip you remember fondly, the feeling you are left with when you think about it, and why.

_____

_____

_____

_____

_____

_____

_____

_____

Your word: _____

8. **Marriage or Dating**: Many lessons are learned in these profound and emotional relationships. Describe the one that impacted you the most.

_____

_____

_____

_____

_____

_____

_____

_____

Your word: _____

9. **Spirituality**: This means many things to many people. Often, beliefs shift over a lifetime. Share a moment when yours shifted, whether slightly or greatly, and why.

_____

_____

_____

_____

_____

_____

_____

_____

Your word: _____

When you have finished this exercise, write the words you identified from the nine experiences above on the template that follows in the corresponding boxes. You can download a copy of this template at solutionariesacademy.com/templates instead if you prefer.

My Life Path

The one positive word that describes my...

CHILDHOOD YEARS

WELCOME TO THE WORLD!

TUMULTUOUS TEENS

These words reflect my authenticity and the wealth of experience and knowledge I bring to the table because they are directly supported by memorable experiences.

WORKING 9–5

FIRST TIME AWAY

BEST FRIEND

TRAVEL

FUTURE

SPIRITUALITY

MARRIAGE OR DATING

Understanding the importance of these words and their backstory will give you the confidence to provide a clear and concise response to the question "Why you?" when you are asked why you are uniquely qualified to lead, to lend support, or to get the job you desire. They reflect your authenticity and the wealth of experience and knowledge you bring to the table because they are directly supported by memorable experiences.

Lesson Three:
Weaving a Richer Fabric

Who inspires you? Chances are it is someone you see as living a big, full life and somehow making a difference in the world.

What inspires you? Perhaps it is a company searching for energy alternatives, cancer cures or connectivity solutions for the isolated in developing nations, or trying to alleviate social issues such as hunger, poverty or gender equality.

We respect and honor visionaries—those who think outside of "the box," sparking possibilities and then fanning the flames so their dreams unfold in the real world. What sets thought leaders apart from the crowd? Quite simply, they take action when others dismiss the seeds of their own great ideas as too grandiose to ever take root.

Some commonly admired traits include: perseverance under adversity, adherence to one's own principles, and making a difference in the lives of others. These traits all boil down to what your values are and you have a pretty good understanding of yours now.

Let's explore a little. Take a moment and list three people who you have not met but who you admire and resonate with. State why you respect them and then narrow each description down to one word.

1. Name: _____
   Reason: _____
   _____

   Word: _____

2. Name: _____
   Reason: _____
   _____

   Word: _____

3. Name: _____
   Reason: _____
   _____

   Word: _____

Identifying people we admire is a key component to self-improvement. It provides us with powerful resources to learn from and be motivated by. When we identify people who have achieved values and goals we care about, we can use them as examples to achieve similar values and goals in our own lives, weaving a richer fabric because of who we are—a fabric with depth and color.

Your life and experiences are no less impressive than Elon Musk's or Oprah's. I suspect if you look at the things you admire the most in people you have a high regard for, you will see you have many of the same deserving qualities. After all, we are drawn to those like us.

But remember, what you see isn't always the whole story. The road is full of twists and turns and everyone has a back-story. Sometimes there is a "halo effect" we need to be cautious about—the tendency to judge them as solely good because they are really good at one thing. We forget they are human like us. They make mistakes and don't always do the right thing.

We really aren't different. Though you may have taken another path, you too have become stronger and wiser. Your toolbox is full of wonderful tools you can use to positively influence others. Remember, people who come in contact with you want to know how you have become the amazing person you are!

Take a minute to study the similarities between the people who you have chosen and you. If the adjectives that are admirable to you don't appear in the words you wrote on your Life Path in Lesson Two, think of how you may have exhibited these traits in the past in some other life experience.

Or better yet, what experiences can you have in the future that will give you the opportunity to acquire these new traits? Our last exercise in this step is to list three meaningful life experiences you would like to have someday and the reason why.

Once again, come up with one word for each that best describes what you hope to gain in terms of values or traits and put the three words in the last box of the *My Life Path* template from Lesson Two ("The Future"). An example might be, "Travel: I would like to travel to Tanzania to work in a girl's school to give them the tools they need to create a bigger life. This would give me a sense of *completion* and deeper *gratitude* for my own gifts."

1. _____ :
   _____
   _____
   _____
   _____

2. _____ :
   _____
   _____
   _____
   _____

3. _____ :

    _____

    _____

    _____

    _____

Remember, what you see is not always what others see. A weaver works from the back of the tapestry, never seeing the front. The colors, in hue and amount, are in reverse of what they will be on the front. Tapestries take a very long time to weave. But with time and sincere effort, more colors and more threads, a complex and rich design emerges. This is your chance to create a design and set an intention to move forward filling in the gaps in your tapestry, weaving an intricate and beautiful pattern.

Step Two

Presenting Yourself to the World with Intention... Brand YOU

Solutionaries reflect the values that are important to them rather than conforming to what they believe others' expectations might be.

Reflect the Authentic You

In Step One, you spent time thinking about people and circumstances that have changed your life and shaped who you are today. You identified qualities and values that have become a part of you through life experiences.

Do you show this very real you to the world or do you find you mask it at times to fit in with your perception of the norm?

In Step Two, you are going to make sure your personal brand reflects your authentic self. After all, how can like-minded peers find you if your special qualities and values don't stand out to the world?

The term "personal branding" is believed to have originally appeared in an article in Fast Company Magazine, where Tom Peters states, "We are CEOs of our own companies: Me, Inc. To be in business today, our most important job is to be head marketer for the brand You."

Today, this analogy appears more important than ever. With careers often becoming more project-based and less linear, we each need to be able to distinguish ourselves in an authentic and unique way from others vying for similar opportunities.

When it comes to your personal brand, you represent yourself all day, every day. If you don't brand yourself first, someone else will. There is very little difference, thanks to social media, between the "work" you and the "real" you. Everyone sees and believes they know a complete picture of who you are. As Jeff

Bezos, founder of Amazon, said "Your brand is what people say about you when you're not in the room."

So, what is your personal brand? It's made up of many things such as your strengths, passions, values and sense of purpose. It's your reputation, whether you have the ability to influence others, the work or cause you are known for, and how people experience you. As Maya Angelou put it, "I've learned that people will forget what you said, people will forget what you did, but people will never forget how you made them feel."

There is no better time than today to realize that you have a brand and need to start managing it. Before you can manage it though, you need to know it. The best way is to develop a clear understanding of the perception others have of you, factor in what you thought the impression you gave others was, and then identify the gaps between the two. That way, you can begin adjusting your brand to what you want it to reflect in the future.

This is no different than the path a business would take to determine how their products or services sit with their customer base or how a human resource department ensures their employer brand is resonating with potential recruits.

What might be a little challenging is willingly listening with an open mind and an open heart as you solicit information. The most important thing to remember is any feedback about the impression you give reflects others' perceptions, not necessarily the truth of who you are. And perception can be tweaked if it feels off to you.

Once you can show others the authentic you, your values and the things that make you unique and special, you will begin attracting a like-minded tribe who want to connect with you and experience all that you are. If things need adjusting, this book will provide you with the knowledge and tools to navigate the change.

So be brave, be open to all comments and input. It's exciting! As Oscar Wilde said, "Be yourself; everyone else is already taken!"

Lesson One:
Eyes Wide Open

We all like to believe that we show ourselves to the world in the best light and most of us make a sincere effort to do so. We often receive conflicting messages—we're told to put our best foot forward while being admonished not to worry about what others think. But if there is one thing we have learned from corporate branding, it is that our personal brand is not like a jacket we put on in the morning and take off at night. It's how we show ourselves to the world when we interact with our family and colleagues, in business meetings and at Friday night happy hours, when we are calm and collected or annoyed and frustrated.

Before you can adjust and tweak your brand, you need to know exactly what it is, not what you think it is. The best way to do this is to ask other people questions with the request that they be frank and honest with you. No penalties attached.

Start your information-gathering task by asking the following questions to at least four people who are a mixture of friends, co-workers and acquaintances. I would suggest you email them these questions so you won't be inclined to ask them to elaborate and they won't be tempted to soften their answers like they might in a verbal exchange. This written format will give them the opportunity to think about the questions quietly and provide you with thoughtful answers.

The more information you gather, the more accurate the final assessment will be.

Brand Survey Questions:

1. What was your first impression of me?

   _____
   _____
   _____
   _____
   _____
   _____
   _____
   _____

2. What skills and talents do you believe I offer—the things that make me unique?

   _____
   _____
   _____
   _____
   _____
   _____
   _____
   _____

3. What do you think my strengths and weaknesses are?

   _____
   _____
   _____
   _____
   _____
   _____
   _____
   _____

4. How does my physical presence show up (i.e., confidence, informality, friendliness)?

5. Does my personal presence differ from my online presence (i.e., LinkedIn, Facebook, Instagram, blogs)?

6. What do you think my values are?

7. Is there a cause or belief I stand for, something I'm passionate about?

_____

_____

_____

_____

_____

_____

_____

_____

8. How do I leave you feeling after I talk with you or have been in your presence?

_____

_____

_____

_____

_____

_____

_____

_____

9. Are you aware of my reputation? What is it?

_____

_____

_____

_____

_____

_____

_____

_____

It takes courage to ask for feedback and be appreciative of it. Just remember, the feedback you receive will allow you to adjust what you reflect to the world if it isn't quite what you had hoped. In many ways, we are mirrors. Nine times out of ten when you smile at someone, they can't help but smile back. If we want more of something, whether it's purpose, income or love, the way we present ourselves to the world is critical. By refining what you present, others with the same goals and desires will be attracted to you.

After you receive the answers, combine them in a statement that says, "Today, I show myself to the world as _____."

This is your current brand and baseline. So, let's go exploring!

Lesson Two:
The Work is in the Gap

Everyone has a story. I try to remind myself of that when people's actions are a mystery to me, when they react in a way I would not, or say things I shake my head at. It is a natural instinct to form an immediate impression of people and situations based on our own experiences—an assumption that may or may not be correct. Whether you like it or not, your personal brand isn't your own impression of who you are, but the combined impressions of other people. Even nameless faces you pass on the street, see at restaurants, at the office, or at a party may convey an unscripted message just by the way they dress or carry themselves. And we have no idea what their backstory is.

When we were kids, my friends and I played a game where we'd pick a couple of strangers who were deep in conversation and then spin a story around the impression they were giving. We never had the nerve to ask them about their real story, but it was fun to imagine. On the TV program, To Tell the Truth, contestants guess which person out of a group is the real individual with a particular story or occupation. Many times, the finalist does not look at all the way one would imagine given what they do. And I am sure we have all been surprised when meeting someone in person after conversing with them on the phone or online, when their physical presence did not match what we had imagined from their voice or words.

If given the opportunity, the best way to stay in alignment with how you are perceived, to make sure it reflects your authentic self, is to let people know who you are by sharing your experiences and the things that are important to you. You can't always do something about snap impressions, but you can begin to build a personal brand through your online presence and personal interactions with people by being conscious of how you present yourself.

In Lesson One of this step, you asked a group of people to tell you about the impression you leave on them to better understand their view of you.

In Lesson Two, you are going to begin looking at the impression you believe you leave to see how it lines up with other people's view of you. It is in the gap that there is room for growth, an opportunity to find ways to show people who you really are as you share your experiences and stories. Ultimately, your circle will grow as more people resonate with you, love and admire all that you are, and want to walk the path with you.

Let's start by having you answer the same questions you posed to people in Lesson One. Keep in mind, you're looking at the impression you believe you leave on others.

1. What is the first impression I make?

_____
_____
_____
_____
_____
_____
_____
_____
_____
_____
_____

2. What do I believe are the skills and talents I demonstrate; the things that make me unique?

_____

_____

_____

_____

_____

_____

_____

_____

_____

3. What do I think I present as my strengths and weaknesses?

_____

_____

_____

_____

_____

_____

_____

_____

_____

4. How does my physical presence show up (i.e., confidence, informality, friendliness)?

_____

_____

_____

_____

_____

_____

_____

5. Does my personal presence differ from my online presence (i.e., LinkedIn, Facebook, Instagram, blogs)?

_____
_____
_____
_____
_____
_____
_____
_____
_____

6. What do others think my values are?

_____
_____
_____
_____
_____
_____
_____
_____

7. Is there a cause or belief others believe I stand for, something I'm passionate about?

_____
_____
_____
_____
_____
_____
_____
_____
_____

8. How do I leave others feeling after I talk with them or have been in their presence?

_____
_____
_____
_____
_____
_____
_____

9. Are they aware of my reputation? What do they think it is?

_____
_____
_____
_____
_____
_____

It's time to do a reality check by filling in the chart that follows (or that you can download at solutionariesacademy.com/templates) to better understand how others perceive you in comparison to how you believe they do. Information is power!

As you look at the responses, do you note any marked differences between your impression and theirs? Now that you have this valuable data, begin to reflect on how you can close the gap by jotting some ideas down in the middle column of the chart.

In Lesson Three, you will begin creating a strategy for "Brand You" to show the world who you really are in a powerful and authentic way. With this newfound consciousness, you will be able to present yourself with intention, attract people and causes that interest you, and understand how important your skills, talents and values are to their success.

Reality Check

	Me	Gap	Them
First Impression			
Skills & Talents			
Strengths			
Weaknesses			
Physical Presence			
Online Presence			
Values			
Cause or Belief			
Feeling or Imprint			

Lesson Three:
Crafting Your Personal Brand

Excavating is hard work! Congratulations on being open and receptive to putting some thought into how you show up in the world. Although it is exciting, it can be intimidating too. We are comfortable in the world as we know it and making shifts, even subtle shifts, takes courage. You chose to take a serious look at your life and experiences because you are hungry for work and a life that fills your emotional reservoir, not just your bank account. You want to collaborate with people who also wish to make a difference in the world and live an exceptional and authentic life.

These initial steps will help you to fulfill that dream. After all, changemakers need to be able to find you when they search for others to work with on projects, advocate for a cause, or provide positive solutions. They will be searching for someone with common interests, hopes and values. Therefore, you need to be visible, both online and in your community. And you must generate interest on their part by answering why they would want to know you.

Great success stories stand out from the crowd. The people in those stories may not have skills or talents any greater than yours, but they communicate the values that resonate with others. When I think of Nelson Mandela and Malala Yousafzai, I think of peacemakers; Mother Theresa, an advocate for the poor or forgotten, and Elizabeth Warren as audacious. When we hear about Apple, we think about innovation, Target as "cheap chic" and Starbucks is equated with consistency. These are all strong positive descriptors and you deserve nothing less.

In Lesson Three, you will begin to craft your Personal Brand Statement (the "what") and your Personal Brand Footprint (the "how") based on the information you have acquired up to this point. This is no time to be humble. Go back and look at the great things your friends and acquaintances have said about you throughout this process and accept them as true!

Personal Brand Statement

Your personal brand statement reflects the heart and soul of who you are and what motivates you. It is important whether you are an entrepreneur, work for a business, or serve as a volunteer. The experiences on your life path have made you who you are and your personal brand statement synthesizes what you stand for. It acts as your North Star in making decisions that are "on brand" so you don't veer off track to off-brand activities. It helps guide you to future experiences you would like to have.

Investing in your personal brand makes you better at what you do and more helpful to others. In other words, find ways to strengthen the very words you claim you are. If you want to show up as giving, then volunteer. If you want others to think you are faithful, then align with spiritual organizations where they can see your involvement. If you want your peers to view you as a mentor, then educate and share. There are no lack of opportunities. You might start by researching local Meetups, conferences and in-person or online classes.

At the end of the day, you need to know how to present who you are, what's important to you, and what you bring to the table, whether you're speaking with a potential employer, a new business partner, a neighborhood board, or a church committee. You demonstrate this through your actions and through sharing stories about your past experiences. In Step One, you identified many significant life stories. These will be important to remember in developing your personal brand statement.

So, let's give it a shot. Start by answering the questions below as a framework. Forget your job title or position description and ask yourself the following questions.

1. What gifts and talents allow you to make a contribution that is remarkable and measurable, with distinct value?

_____

_____

_____

_____

_____

_____

_____

_____

_____

_____

2. What are you most proud of that you can take credit for?

_____

_____

_____

_____

_____

_____

_____

_____

_____

_____

3. What reputational values are important to you?

_____
_____
_____
_____
_____
_____
_____
_____
_____

4. What would you like to be known for, no matter how grandiose or far-fetched it may seem today?

_____
_____
_____
_____
_____
_____
_____
_____
_____

With those answers in mind, it's time to try writing your own branding statement. Below is an example of a personal brand statement that may help you develop yours. It starts with an action verb to show others you are moving toward a goal with a vision in hand. It also conveys how you will go about reaching your goal and the boundaries within which you operate.

To (*what you want to do, achieve, become*) so (*reasons why it is important*). I will do this by (*specific behaviors or actions you can use to get there*).

I value (*choose one to three values*) because (*reasons why these values are important to you*). Accordingly, I will (*what you can do to live by these values*).

For example, "To be the most sought-after entrepreneur in the organic food business, while striving to provide my customers with the healthiest products they deserve. I value integrity, fair pricing and the finest quality ingredients. I will strive to be the best in class and an industry leader at all times."

My Personal Brand Statement

_____
_____
_____
_____
_____
_____
_____
_____
_____
_____

Personal Brand Footprint

If you're interested in becoming a leader in your field, landing your dream job, or showing your expertise in a particular area, you need to put some thought into where your brand statement appears and the effect it has.

Your imprint is reflected in your personal relationships and online presence. Who makes up your network? Is it friends and family, social media sites like Facebook, Instagram or Twitter, networking options like LinkedIn, or special interest groups that resonate with you?

Whether you inspire your network or others find you intolerable to work with, I guarantee you have an influence (be it positive or negative) you may not be fully aware of.

Let's take a look at your radius of influence.

1. Identify the people you impact every day with your personal brand, whether for good or bad.

   _____

   _____

   _____

   _____

   _____

   _____

   _____

   _____

   _____

   _____

2. Google yourself to review your digital footprint. Describe your current online presence based on the search results you find.

   _____

   _____

   _____

   _____

   _____

   _____

   _____

   _____

   _____

3. After reviewing your overall presence, look at the items below and ask yourself whether your personal brand statement is accurately reflected in them, if you have them. Don't just answer "yes" or "no." Describe how the reader is given the opportunity to know a three-dimensional you. If you believe an item may need some revision to add depth and color, begin to think about ways you will make that happen and note how you can begin to revise them.

Your marketing collateral

Resume, bio or cover letters: Do you tell your story through attached testimonials, use a video bio where they can see and connect with you, list the skills that set you apart, or specify what you bring to the table that is different?

_____
_____
_____
_____
_____
_____
_____

Business cards: Is the back blank with space for the person receiving it to write notes? Does it have a memorable photo or tagline about you or list particular skills?

_____
_____
_____
_____
_____
_____

Website: Is your brand identified through visual images such as pictures, colors, fonts? Does it tell stories about what you stand for and the work you are here to do?

_____
_____
_____
_____
_____
_____

Your field of expertise

Your blog: Do you show your professional expertise or share knowledge based on your life experiences or work and educational experience with those it might help? Do you support other blogs in the same interest space by connecting with them and encouraging them?

_____
_____
_____
_____
_____
_____
_____

Webinars: Are you being helpful to others by sharing your knowledge? Are you showing up at other webinars that are of interest to you to find a community of like-minded people?

_____
_____
_____
_____
_____
_____

Trade or industry publications: Do you share what you know with your peers? This is a perfect way to show hard-earned expertise.

_____
_____
_____
_____
_____
_____

Posts on LinkedIn: Do you connect daily with at least one like-minded business colleague, join special interest groups, share your thoughts in your posts, and support others in theirs?

_____

_____

_____

_____

_____

_____

Podcast interviews: Have you found a group of like-minded individuals whose cause you support by listening to their podcasts? Even commenting or asking questions shows you care and are engaged. And others will see you as a tribe member and may reach out to you to contribute as well.

_____

_____

_____

_____

_____

_____

Speaking engagements: Do you tell your story to others? Often speaking engagements are captured on video and can be uploaded to your website, LinkedIn, or Facebook to show you have an expertise or a story to tell.

_____

_____

_____

_____

_____

_____

Appearance: Lastly, don't forget your physical presentation. Consider your grooming, body language, clothing and appearance, as they all are representative of your personal brand and message. Remember, nonverbal tools are as important as verbal. What adjustments can you make so you reflect trustworthiness, subject matter expertise, confidence and efficiency at first glance? If you need a little help to get started, I have provided some suggestions at solutionariesacademy.com/bonuses. Just look for the First Impression Tip Sheet.

_____

_____

_____

_____

_____

_____

Looking Forward

As you expand your network, begin to think about the types of people or companies you would like to attract and how you will go about doing that. Choose three of the most significant ideas you identified above and commit over the next quarter to growing your footprint and solidifying your personal brand through these avenues.

1. _____

2. _____

3. _____

Step Three

Visualizing Possibilities as a Change Architect

Solutionaries envision a better world and are willing to go on a transformative adventure.

Trust the Magic
of New Beginnings

You have been doing a lot of reaching back and pulling forward in the first two steps of this book. In the process, you have identified values you have learned and adopted throughout your life that complement the skills and talents you use daily. You have also studied how you present all of these qualities to others in your personal and business interactions, both offline and online, and how you are perceived. More importantly, you have considered how to manage what you project so you can find and attract kindred spirits with the same goals, aspirations and values.

In Step Three, you will identify exciting new innovations or trends that interest you, and causes and issues that bother you—ones you wish were resolved and were a thing of the past.

Every day, we are barraged with information about some of the world's most pressing issues. It can be overwhelming and difficult to imagine how we can personally contribute to fixing them. With so much digital overload, it can be challenging to narrow our focus to one particular issue we resonate with and feel a desire to contribute to. It's even worse if we are made to feel like there is something wrong with us if we cannot readily name our passion or purpose.

The concept of "passion" or "purpose" is a daunting idea for many who are just trying to navigate life's daily challenges, while keeping the bills paid and the family safe.

Though it may feel like something is missing, there just never seems to be enough time to figure out what it is. While some never questioned their innate certainty about the road they would take, clear from childhood, for most, it shows up as a product of life experiences. If you have been searching, the steps that follow will help you.

First, let's figure out what resonates with your heart, mind and spirit. One of the best ways to do this is by creating a clarity map that will provide a visual aid and daily reminder of these very things.

For the moment, be less concerned with financial well-being than spiritual and emotional abundance. You are searching for the issues that touch your heart. Often, we are told if we find our "heart work," financial abundance will follow. I personally believe it to be true.

The clarity map you will create in this step is different than the vision boards you may have created in the past. It differs because, rather than being a tool for visualizing and manifesting, this is a tool to be used while you are still excavating, looking for that special gem that will give you joy and fulfillment and make your life more meaningful. It's the precursor to the vision board you may want to create once you're done with this workbook and have more clarity about the direction you would like to go and what you would like to manifest.

So, let's go treasure hunting!

Lesson One:
It's How, Not What, You See

The goal of the clarity map is to help you get unstuck. In a world where we face digital overload daily and what often seems like insurmountable problems around the planet, it can be hard to see where we can contribute in a meaningful way. It is easy to feel somewhat paralyzed with inaction, feeling small and helpless against their magnitude.

For many in the Baby Boomer generation, age can feel like a tremendous burden when, in reality, their wisdom is badly needed. Millennials with a deep desire to serve and savvy technological skills may understand how to reach the faceless millions but lack a network of proven leaders, mentors and funders. The one thing both generations are clear about is they each want to contribute. Often, they just aren't sure how and where to begin.

A few of the challenges facing our planet and mankind, as a species, are: healthcare, food shortages, climate change, poverty, energy, addiction, education and equal rights. It is clear there is much to be done by all of us. Some issues will get us fired up emotionally, inspiring us and motivating us to help. Others, not so much. Often, if the topic touches us, we can trace our connection with it to one of our life experiences or perhaps that of a friend or family member.

As you begin sifting through the multitude of concerns, it is common to rely on your personal filters to distill the list to ones you can relate to. For example, you may have been raised with a certain problem, such as abusive or alcoholic parents or poverty, which set off certain triggers. Or you may be offended by certain words or behaviors, such as discrimination or bullying, and feel angry about them.

Sometimes, our viewpoints may be pretty myopic about certain things as a result of our own experiences. In many cases, we either obsess about ways we can resolve them or ignore them because they are too painful to look at.

I have been told by many people that when they look at the news and the unthinkable tragedies around the world, they find they look away because of the sadness they feel when they confront them head on. But look and feel we must, we are Solutionaries and the world needs us!

What if your view was unfiltered? Would it give you the ability to step back and see a resolution more clearly? Would you be able to view issues you did not relate to before with fresh eyes?

Before you start the process of creating your clarity map, take time to answer the questions below. Remember, this information is only for you. So put some thought into your answers and be as straightforward and honest as you can be.

1. Describe the filters you use when you hear about a particular social issue like the ones listed below (i.e., these things happen to them, not me; I've never known anyone who did not have enough food; people who are homeless just haven't tried to find a job; people who claim racism or sexual harassment are just acting like victims; I choose not to look at the news anymore because it's too confusing or depressing and just makes me feel helpless).

   Homelessness: _____

   Hunger: _____

   Equal Rights: _____

Racism: _____

Guns: _____

_____ :_____

_____ :_____

2. For each of the above issues, close your eyes for a moment and imagine yourself stepping into the shoes of those challenged with that particular issue. Does this new vantage point help you better understand their perspective? Do you have a sense of resistance or stubbornness about changing "sides," even if it's just in your mind? Why?

_____

_____

_____

_____

_____

_____

_____

_____

_____

3. What personal experience have you had with a pressing issue such as hunger, addiction, homelessness, natural disaster, health or emotional problems, or a local community concern? If you can't think of any, what sets you apart?

_____

_____

_____

_____

_____

_____

_____

_____

_____

4. What beliefs did your parents pass on to you that you questioned? What did you do differently?

    _____
    _____
    _____
    _____
    _____
    _____
    _____
    _____
    _____
    _____
    _____

5. Our perspective on life can show up as an attitude that dictates whether you believe your life is a diverse tapestry of extraordinary moments, a mundane existence, or something in between. How would you describe your perspective and the lens through which you view life? Are you grateful, naïve, bored, positive, cynical or unfulfilled?

    _____
    _____
    _____
    _____
    _____
    _____
    _____
    _____
    _____
    _____
    _____

We exist in a time where our communities are divided. Our points of view on everything from climate change to politics are raw and often distorted by our personal interpretations or those we have adopted from the media, our fears and opinions. These are then colored by our experience of religion, ethics, personal relationships, work and school.

Can we find consensus or at least shift a few degrees to better understand the root of the problems we wish no longer existed? This may be the first step to creating positive change.

Lesson Two:
Without a Map, Any Road Will Do

It's time to start designing your clarity map. This map is a record of the things you are discovering throughout this process and a visual representation of how they tie together. I have prepared a template you will find on the next page, which will act as a guide and show you where to place words and pictures that remind you of:

- **Your core values** and those you want to strengthen. (*Step One*)

- **Your personal brand** and how you will enhance it both offline and online. (*Step Two*)

- **The causes** that inspire, motivate and interest you. (*Step Three*)

- **Your "tribe"**—in other words, the companies and individuals in your area of interest. (*Step Four*)

- **The value exchange** between you and the organizations or individuals who need you. (*Step Five*)

- **Your vision** for the resolution of a problem and how you plan to help. (*Step Six*)

A copy of the template can also be downloaded from solutionariesacademy.com/templates.

Clarity Map

MY CORE VALUES
and those I want to
strengthen
(Step 1)

**MY PERSONAL
BRAND**
and how I will
enhance it
(Step 2)

MY VISION
and how I plan
to help
(Step 6)

MY INTERESTS
and the causes that
inspire me
(Step 3)

MY VALUE MATCHES
and the organizations
that align with the
skills I offer
(Step 5)

MY TRIBE
and the people
who interest me
(Step 4)

_____   _____

Signature   Date

In addition to adding the words, concepts and tasks you have discovered and committed to in Steps One and Two, you will continue to add to your map as you engage in this process of exploration. Your map is a living visual aid and will change with new experiences and revelations.

To get started, you will need the following supplies:

- Old magazines
- Photos or color photocopies of yourself
- A glue stick, Elmer's or Tacky Glue
- A large poster board
- Crayons, colored pencils or markers
- Scissors
- Colored, shiny or metallic paper
- Decorative accessories such as stickers, glue-on stars or rhinestones

This is a creative project, so make it fun! The first thing to do is glue your picture smack dab in the middle of the poster board. After all, this is your story. Then, using the clarity map template to guide you in your exploration, start with a stack of magazines that are focused on current events or particular industries or trends that interest you and look for images or words that catch your imagination and represent causes that attract you or concern you.

Magazines are expensive, but libraries give them away and stores like Half Priced Books are good sources of inexpensive materials. Pictures printed off the internet are a good option though you run the risk of going down the internet rabbit hole.

Find pictures or words for each of the following topics you feel drawn to and cut them out. They can apply to a local issue or something on a global scale and may be subsets of bigger topics (i.e., homelessness might be a subset of poverty or healthcare, gay rights would be a subset of equal rights, etc.).

In addition to the list I have provided to you below, find a few more topics that catch your attention.

- Poverty

- Innovation

- Human Rights

- Environment

- _____

- _____

- _____

Out of the pictures you have selected, choose the three topics that speak to your heart the most and glue the pictures on your clarity map in the space provided for Step Three materials. These are the things you most wish were behind us and a thing of the past or some amazing new innovation you hope will happen.

Now, find words to show that you are part of the solution (i.e. advocate, leader, designer, fundraiser) even if they seem wishful and not real at the moment. Glue them in the space designated by your picture as if you were currently experiencing these things.

Relax. Let go and surrender worry and any feelings of perfectionism about the map. There are no rules. You can fill it up, leave lots of open space, or decorate it with whimsical items if you choose. Have fun and create your own collage to remind you of just how valuable you are, the things that touch your heart, and why and how you are part of the answer.

Once again, don't forget to add pictures and words from your Step One and Two answers in the spots designated. You will continue adding additional items to your clarity map throughout this process.

When it is completed, you will sign and date it on the bottom. As you are working on your clarity map, take time to enjoy and admire it, while appreciating your newfound clearness. Place it in an area where you can easily see it when you do your meditation, affirmation or visualization exercises. You might hang it by your bed, by your desk, on a mirror, or in a room where you spend a lot of time.

To get the maximum benefits from your clarity map, look at it and focus on it for about ten minutes twice a day and project yourself into the pictures that show you and your tribe as Solutionaries creating amazing change and making a positive impact on those around you. This will help you keep your interest and enthusiasm level high, which projects to those around you, both in person and online. When you lose the image, open your eyes and try this process again. And don't forget... *The greatest value of a picture is when it forces us to notice what we never expected to see!*

Lesson Three:
With Courage Comes Clarity

In Lesson Two of this step, you took a look at socially pressing issues—ones affecting a considerable number of individuals—and discovered topics of interest and concern to you. You then filtered them down to a list of three for your clarity map.

In Lesson Three, you will examine the relationship between those topics and your life experiences. Although, you may not see an immediate association, I guarantee you something connected both your heart and mind to the concerns and topics you identified. Before you try to figure out the connection, let's do a little research and learn more about the subjects that drew you.

In the spaces below, write the issue that either interested you or concerned you and why you chose it. Make sure it is a narrow topic brought down to its lowest common denominator. For example, rather than putting hunger as a topic, you might list poor crop yield, over-fishing, food dumping or food aid. Rather than putting education, you might list literacy, school lunch programs, dropout rates or bullying.

Once you have identified your topic, add the additional filters of geography (i.e., neighborhood, city, county). In other words, although the problem may be global, your goal is to connect it to a community issue if possible, one in which you can ultimately participate locally with your tribe as a changemaker.

Begin to research how it affects your network and your community by spending time identifying some of the key stakeholders and innovations being implemented to solve the problems. These days the world is at your fingertips thanks to the internet. Those you have identified may be out of your geographical area but may have a group of committed and inspired followers relatively close to home.

As you go through this process, complete the questions below. You should list names (individuals or organizations) and describe their efforts in detail. In particular, why did they get involved with this issue? What sparked their passion? Who is their tribe of supporters? Is their work making an impact? What are their challenges—the things they need to overcome to be successful in finding a resolution?

After you have done this research, ask yourself if you, or anyone you know, have been impacted by or had a similar experience to the market these changemakers are trying to serve? If yes, tell your story in detail.

Many times, it takes courage to voice that you can relate to a group that needs to be served, as we are often concerned this will make us look like a victim or "one of them." But the concept of serving while receiving is what creates the yin and yang of balance and allows us to be more fully present and informed as we find common ground and ultimate answers.

Topic 1: _____

Location: _____

Individuals or Organizations: _____

_____

_____

(a) Where they are located: _____

_____

_____

(b) What they are doing: _____
_____
_____

(c) How and why they got involved:_____
_____
_____

(d) Is their tribe yours? How do you know?_____
_____
_____

(e) Their challenges: _____
_____
_____

(f) Ways you can add value: _____
_____
_____

Your Story/Relationship:_____
_____
_____
_____
_____

Topic 2:_____
Location: _____
Individuals or Organizations: _____
_____

(a) Where they are located: _____
_____
_____

(b) What they are doing: _____
_____
_____

(c) How and why they got involved:_____

_____

_____

(d) Is their tribe yours? How do you know?_____

_____

_____

(e) Their challenges: _____

_____

_____

(f) Ways you can add value: _____

_____

_____

Your Story/Relationship:_____

_____

_____

_____

_____

Topic 3:_____
Location: _____
Individuals or Organizations: _____

_____

(a) Where they are located: _____

_____

_____

(b) What they are doing: _____

_____

_____

(c) How and why they got involved:_____

_____

_____

(d) Is their tribe yours? How do you know?_____

_____

_____

(e) Their challenges: _____

_____

(f) Ways you can add value: _____

_____

_____

Your Story/Relationship:_____

_____

_____

_____

_____

It takes courage to connect in a deep way with something or someone you might not be sure you relate to, even if you feel compelled to fix a problem. But with courage comes clarity and the knowledge that your schooling is never complete. Understanding your biases, limitations and deep-rooted connections improves your understanding of the world around you and allows you to use what you have learned to be in service to others.

Most people did not wake up with a burning desire to change the status quo. Rather, there was an incident in their lives that made them look a little closer and seek to fix a problem that had affected them, a loved one or a greater population.

These changemakers generally have certain things in common. When they saw something that agitated and disturbed them, they made an effort to get to the root of the issue and understand the contributing factors. They wanted to fix it so life as they knew it would be different for themselves and others. They were generous with their knowledge and talents and sought out the wisdom of the collective, building mutually supportive relationships benefiting all.

You are a changemaker and Solutionary and a critical part of this universal "team!"

Step Four

Identifying, Finding and Engaging Your Tribe

*Solutionaries believe the force
of social innovation is built
through collaboration
and shared wisdom.*

The Power of Collective Wisdom

One of the most fundamental human needs is the need to belong. We all want to feel loved and accepted by others. We want work that makes us feel worthy with peers who respect and genuinely appreciate us. Often, these needs are met when we become part of a group of people who share common interests and values. A synergy is generated allowing them to create something much greater than any of them could have designed individually.

As the founder of the nonprofit WGN Global Fund, I have witnessed the power of a common vision in the world of microfinance. Women get together in groups of twelve to support each other in their businesses. They co-sign on a pooled loan, all responsible for keeping each woman accountable to their business and the payback of the debt. Their vision is for a better life for their families and for themselves. In my Collective I Leadership program for teen girls, my hope is to teach them that it is no longer about the individual "I." Rather, today we live in a world of the "collective I," where each of us can stand alone in our individuality but appreciate and thrive more fully in a world where the collective wisdom of all is pooled.

Aspen trees provide a unique model of connection. They grow in a community that shares a common root and nutrient system, and their population is healthiest when made up of trees at all levels of maturity, relying on each other to subsist. Even if a tree dies, the root system remains intact, sending up replacements nearby, which is why they are the first to repopulate after a fire. They were considered the largest living organism on the planet with one organization exceeding 100 acres in size, every tree connected, every tree sharing.

We, in fact, are just as connected. We are healthiest when our entire community is well and living in abundance—knowing we can rely on each other for sustenance and support.

It is well acknowledged that positive relationships have an enormous influence on our overall well-being, and mental health is a significant component of this. The World Health Organization (WHO) defines positive mental health as a "state of well-being in which individuals realize their potential, cope with the normal stresses of life, work productively and fruitfully, and make a contribution to her or his community." One of the most fulfilling ways to do this is to work and play with people whom you can support and who support you.

In this step, you are going to locate individuals and organizations with the same values, visions and goals as yours. You will identify the qualities of a perfect fit and then define a strategy for finding that group and engaging with them.

Lesson One:
Envision Your Tribe

In Lesson One, you are going to contemplate your tribe—the community you long to belong to. It might be made up of people who appreciate you just as you are or it might be composed of people who support your dreams. This group of people will encourage you to pursue your goals, offering you a sense of kinship through difficult times and gratitude when you succeed. They are the cheerleaders who recharge you, celebrate with you and inspire you, their eyes lighting up when you tell them about your dreams and ambitions. And they act as the guards who hold a place for your vision, commiserating with you in challenging times. They are your peeps!

Today, you probably belong to more than one group bound together by education, occupation, religion, political beliefs, local community involvement or hobbies. But not all of them provide the emotional support we need, which is what sets a tribe apart. Having a tight-knit support group, one that offers emotional safety and security, is the result of a give-and-take relationship. So think about ways you can ensure your interactions are two-way—as you receive, you also give. One of the most fulfilling aspects of our lives is when we give back to others in our circle and in our communities.

Answer the following questions about specific groups within your topic of interest that attract you. Do this exercise for at least three different groups.

First, identify the type of group (i.e., work, hobbies, social, educational, health and well-being etc.) and then consciously envision the perfect tribe for you. Remember, the people who you associate with impact every facet of your life from your income to your happiness. We are who we hang out with. Happiness is contagious and negativity is a downer. Your vibe attracts your tribe.

Over the last few steps, you have carefully taken a look at how you present yourself to the world. Now, more than ever, keep that in mind as it will be important to finding the connection you hope for:

Type of group: _____

Area of interest: _____

1. What qualities do you want in the members?

_____

_____

_____

_____

_____

2. What do you hope to get out of this group?

_____

_____

_____

_____

_____

_____

3. What would you like to give this group?

_____

_____

_____

_____

_____

4. How do you think this group will inspire and motivate you?

_____

_____

_____

_____

_____

_____

5. How will you lift up others in the group and encourage its members?

_____

_____

_____

_____

_____

_____

_____

6. What do you expect to learn from the group?

_____

_____

_____

_____

_____

_____

_____

7. How will you help others to grow in the group?

_____

_____

_____

_____

_____

_____

_____

8. How do you envision the group rejoicing and applauding times you feel successful?

_____
_____
_____
_____
_____
_____

9. How will you help others to celebrate their victories?

_____
_____
_____
_____
_____
_____

10. How often would you like to connect with this group?

_____
_____
_____
_____
_____
_____

Remember, as Rumi said, "Set your life on fire. Seek those who fan your flames." I would add that you too can, and should be, the wind beneath other's wings. It's exciting to think about a bonfire of transformational change, isn't it?

Lesson Two:
Find Your Tribe

Waiting for people who are interested in the same things you are to find you is a no-win proposition. Like anything else worthwhile, you must show up and be willing to let others know you are available and ready to participate.

In Lesson One of this step, you spent time thinking about the tribe you would like to either grow or bring into your life.

Over the last few steps, you have articulated values that are important to you and examined how you show up in the world. You have also identified things that are important to you or that bother you.

Armed with all of this information, you are ready to go on a search for people and companies with values and common goals aligned with yours.

There are many ways to search for communities of like-minded people. Thanks to the internet, geographical location is no longer a limitation and your search for people and companies with the same interests is relatively easy. People are also able to meet each other on Zoom, Skype and Facetime calls, which make the connections more personal than an email, text or a simple phone call.

I guarantee that in addition to your local search for a network, there is an online community out there filled with like-minded people anxious to meet others who share their interests.

Some examples of ways to find your tribe are:

- Start a networking group.
- Get together with peers to mastermind your businesses.
- Plan a retreat together with others interested in exploring a common topic.
- Take a class or sign up for a workshop.
- Attend a lecture at a university, museum or cultural exposition.
- Go to a trade show in the sector that interests you.
- Support charity events, volunteer or serve on a board or committee.
- Participate in environmental cleanup days or help with Earth Day activities.
- Mentor entrepreneurs through SCORE or other incubators.
- Volunteer to lead corporate social responsibility programs at your place of business.
- Find a spiritual community that feels authentic and inspires you.
- Research Meetup groups with a common interest or register for community events on Eventbrite.
- Join online groups, such as Yahoo, Facebook, Google Hangouts, MEETin, GroupSpaces, LinkedIn, Instagram and Twitter, to research the topics, activities and locations you're interested in.
- Explore apps that connect people with common interests, such as Hitch, nTANgo, Brigge, Zumpout, Opin, Smacktive, Glynk or Wegodo.
- Start a blog on a subject that interests you and

comment on other blogs, perhaps offering to feature someone else's blog.

- Sign up for Google alerts about topics or people that interest you so you can stay connected to what is going on with your tribe.

Once you have identified the groups that attract you, you must actually present yourself to others you don't know. For some, this can be hard. Even adults can feel like kids when stepping outside of their comfort zone.

I can still remember when my father taught me how to shake hands with another person, instructing me to put my right hand out and firmly grip the other person's hand to show them I was genuinely interested in them. Nine times out of ten, they were adults and much bigger than me, but somehow even at that age I felt like I was stepping up—and I was!

Make the first move by showing the true you, not a manufactured version of what you think might be attractive to others. You have spent time weaving your values into your bio and resume, your social media presence and your website if you have one. It should be easy for others to see and understand who you really are and form an authentic relationship with you.

In Lesson One, you imagined the characteristics of three particular groups or tribes you would like to bring into your life.

In Lesson Two, you will research and write down a specific organization you have identified for each of those groups and answer the following questions. Use the same thought process you would if you were looking for a service opportunity, potential business partners or the perfect rewarding job.

I'm confident you will find a group of like-minded individuals who will become colleagues sharing a common goal of ensuring the success of the project organization and your success as a contributor.

Group or Organization: _____

1. Why are you attracted to this organization? Why do you believe they are part of your tribe?

    _____
    _____
    _____
    _____
    _____
    _____
    _____

2. What social issue do they address and how are they doing it?

    _____
    _____
    _____
    _____
    _____
    _____
    _____
    _____

3. What benefit or support do you hope to receive from this organization?

    _____
    _____
    _____
    _____
    _____
    _____
    _____
    _____

4. What needs can you fill for them? Will you volunteer, try to seek employment with them, or align as a business partner?

_____

_____

_____

_____

_____

_____

5. How and when will you contact them initially? How will you stay connected?

_____

_____

_____

_____

_____

_____

6. How much time are you willing to commit to the group?

_____

_____

_____

_____

_____

I heard once that you can't start the next chapter if you keep re-reading the last one. To move forward from the "flatness" so many of you have told me you feel, it's time to take that first step into the unknown.

Any time we search out a new adventure or experience, it can be exciting but also a little unnerving. It's easier to reflect and do research online sometimes than to actually move out into the community and participate but that is our next step. So, take a deep breath and let's go!

Lesson Three:
Connect with Your Tribe

We all like to be around people who support us in our highest good—people who want the very best for us. Yet relationships are only fulfilling when they go both ways— when they are mutually satisfying and we give as much as we receive. There are many ways you can engage and support others in your communities. Often, the most important ways to connect might seem like the most obvious.

Do you smile and make eye contact? Do you address people by their name (i.e., make a note of their name tags or repeat it after they share it with you) and speak in a friendly manner? Are you fully present with them, your body language open? Are you thoughtful with good manners? Are you a reflection of truthfulness and accountability? Do you offer empathy and compassion?

The list is endless but it all boils down to treating others the way you hope to be treated. Are you compatible, kindred spirits who respect each other with a shared interest in the common good?

If you are trying to strengthen personal contacts, you might consider working with others on a project with meaning to everyone, such as volunteer work in your community, planting a communal garden, or cooking a batch of weekly meals together. Once you connect with people, talk to them... Really talk to them. Ask questions and listen to the answers. Be relatable and vulnerable. Share your losses as well as your wins. Look for the bonds when it might seem there are none.

In addition to strong personal relationships, good working relationships are important for many reasons. You spend a large portion of time with the people you work with, so if the relationship is positive, work will be more enjoyable. You are also likely to get more done than if you are wasting time and energy overcoming problems. Furthermore, these relationships are critical to the success of your career, positive reviews, endorsements and new opportunities. Vibrant and respected dealings with customers, suppliers and other key stakeholders are essential to your success at your place of work.

Take time to think about ways you can strengthen important relationships and attract positive new ones by answering the questions below:

1. **Developing your people skills:** Listening and responding in a way that makes the other person feel heard goes a long way in establishing mutually respectful relationships. Do you communicate effectively, getting the results you hope for? Do you listen intently to others and relate to them? Would training help develop these critical skills?

_____

_____

_____

_____

_____

_____

_____

_____

_____

2. **Speaking positively about others:** Showing support of your co-workers and your boss, rather than negative talk, demonstrates that you are a team player. Are you caught up in office gossip or have you established boundaries? Do you proceed with caution on social media or proceed with unfiltered posts? Do others feel safe in your commentary?

_____
_____
_____
_____
_____
_____
_____
_____
_____
_____

3. **Showing appreciation:** Do you tell people thank you using handwritten notes or personalized email and lift them up for their efforts? Do you endorse them on platforms such as LinkedIn, give them a "like" on Facebook, or send a kudos to the Human Resources department to be placed in their files? How do you boost your colleagues' morale?

_____
_____
_____
_____
_____
_____
_____
_____
_____
_____

SOLUTIONARIES • Step Four

4. **Attending company social events:** Do you go to the company parties, picnics and happy hours and actively meet other colleagues from your company rather than just hibernating with a few from your department? Do you follow up afterwards to learn more over coffee or a quick meet-and-greet? Do you include "newbies" into your work projects?

_____

_____

_____

_____

_____

_____

_____

_____

5. **Scheduling time to give back:** Helping others achieve their goals by offering access to information and resources they might need shows you are a team player and diligent mentor. You might offer guidance over coffee or lunch. Equally helpful can be connecting coworkers or others with common interests or following up with other resources that might be helpful. Often, it seems like the amount of time we have in our lives is shrinking and it can be hard to find ways to make the extra time. If that is the case for you, I have some suggestions on scheduling in the Mining for Time tip sheet at solutionariesacademy.com/bonuses.

_____

_____

_____

_____

_____

_____

_____

_____

Throughout this step, you have thought carefully about the organizations you would like to align with and why. You have considered the value you can provide to them and what you will receive in return.

Now it's time to get specific with an action plan covering how you will connect with these groups. Below list three organizations or groups you will associate with. Then list some specific ways you will engage with the members of those groups.

Group One: _____

_____

_____

_____

_____

_____

_____

_____

Group Two: _____

_____

_____

_____

_____

_____

_____

_____

Group Three: _____

_____

_____

_____

_____

_____

_____

_____

Just a reminder! It's time to add your tribe to your clarity map. Include adjectives describing how you will find and engage them. As you look at your map, this will be a daily reminder and keep you vigilant and committed to your search.

Step Five

Matching Values

Solutionaries share a common vision of a better world.

Aligning Your Values to Ensure Success

S tep Five provides an additional filtering process that will enable you to take the information you have accumulated and hone in on the organizations you are best suited to serve or, if you are an entrepreneur, to ensure the peers you have identified have values aligned with yours.

During our time together, you have:

- Reviewed the values you have adopted along your life path.

- Inspected how you present those values to the world.

- Identified the issues that interest or bother you.

- Researched the stakeholders actively working to make the issues a thing of the past.

Throughout each step you have collected and condensed information into meaningful words and actionable tasks. You can now move forward with clarity to find work that fills your emotional reservoir and partners you with people who will inspire and motivate you.

The tribe of changemakers you have identified is probably a pretty good size. To ensure you are a good match, you will want to make sure that not only your interests, talents and skills align, but also your values. The chances of long-term success in any partnership or working relationship are increased when the partners' values support and complement each other.

In Lesson One of this step, you will create and write out your own vision, mission and values statements. This is a deeper dive than Step Two where you looked at your personal brand in terms of how you present yourself to the world physically and digitally. Just as a company's business strategy uses their core statements as their guideposts and framework, so should you. Adding these layers of information allows you to show up with conviction and clarity of purpose.

As you narrow the field of who you would like to team up with, you need to make sure you have a clear understanding of "Company You" to present to "Company Them."

Therefore, in Lesson Two, you will take a look at the foundational pillars in the organizations you identified in the previous step. You will review their vision, mission and values statements, research how they implement their goals, explore how they show up in the world, and ultimately decide whether they "walk the talk." Armed with this information, you will be able to determine the commonalities you share.

And finally, in Lesson Three, you will see how this information fits into your present working environment. Some of you, not wanting to leave your current job but anxious for your employer to reflect its commitment to social innovation, will be interested in taking a look at the value exchange between your company and its stakeholders (i.e., prospective employees, customers and vendors). Is the business sustainable and an innovative contributor to the common good?

This presents an opportunity to think about ways the organization can add value to the community, enhance the value exchange with its employees, or become more environmentally conscious.

Or you may be considering starting your own socially conscious business and thinking about its foundational pillars and the types of employees and partners with whom you want to align. Either way, the following exercises will form a good roadmap as you begin to formulate your new business concept or study the foundation and workings of your present organization.

Ultimately, we all want the same thing—to make a difference and for others to see the value in us and the services we provide.

Lesson One:
The Three Pillars of
"Company You"

The Three Pillars of "Company You"

Before you can move forward, you need a clear understanding of the framework you will operate within to ensure you stay focused and on track. Just as any business has vision, mission and values statements, so should "Company You."

As you write them, you will want to make sure they each stand on their own individually, as well as collectively, in a well-synchronized set. These statements define your personal credo, forming a three-legged stool of support and reinforcement. So how do they differ?

The "Why"

Visionaries think big. They are a source of inspiration to all those around them. Your vision statement should reflect your hopes and desires to make a difference in the world in a particular way—to imagine what is possible for the community you want to serve. It will be up to you to hold the vision like a beacon of light on the horizon for those you bring on your journey with you. Without a vision, why do the work? It's like a ship without a rudder.

The "What"

The mission statement outlines the actual work you must do to get to the ultimate destination. This includes basic business plans or strategic roadmaps that pave a way to reach your goal. We often see companies that have mistakenly crafted empty combined mission/vision statements that simply say they are focused on the quality of services of manufactured goods or telling the world they aspire to be best in class. Statements like these offer no guideposts or framework for those trying to implement the work and fall flat for anyone reading them.

Your mission statement is not just talk. It is your walk and the path forward.

The "How"

At the beginning of this workbook, you drafted your values statement, the third pillar of your foundation for success. It expresses your core values and sets boundaries within which you will execute your mission to reach your vision. It is a framework that supports necessary and appropriate decisions, especially critical when clarity is not readily at hand. It is the "how" that must travel with the "why" and the "what," reflecting the core principles within which you operate.

All three of these statements need to form the foundation and criteria of every decision you make. They are part of each day as sure as that first cup of coffee or first customer call, steady and predictable.

A Powerful Combination

Once you have nailed down these three statements, you will be able to begin work on your next steps within the framework and structure of your vision, mission and values. It is critical that you make sure they do not repeat themselves or give conflicting messages. Each must stand on its own for the purpose it is intended, but work collectively to complete the set. They are the guideposts you will use to begin to reframe your work and social giveback strategy, so be sure to refer to them regularly.

Let's get started fine-tuning yours using the exercises that follow. If you find yourself struggling to come up with enough action or value words, I have provided a Values Master List that may be helpful at solutionariesacademy.com/bonuses.

Your Vision Statement

Your vision statement is a concise but memorable and inspirational summary that describes the positive impact and legacy you want to make. It will be your compass that keeps you, and others you bring on your journey, focused.

You now have clarity about causes that inspire or bother you and an idea of how you can participate as a Solutionary. Take time to answer the questions below so you can craft a vision statement you and your tribe can relate to. Dreaming big is a must!

1. What is your inspiration and dream for "Company You?"

    _____
    _____
    _____
    _____
    _____
    _____

2. What is the cause behind your dream?

    _____
    _____
    _____
    _____
    _____
    _____

3. How do you feel when you think about your vision?

_____

_____

_____

_____

_____

_____

_____

4. Is there anything unique about your dream that sets it apart from others' or is your dream part of a larger movement?

_____

_____

_____

_____

_____

_____

_____

5. What mental image do you cause others to conjure up when you tell them your dream?

_____

_____

_____

_____

_____

_____

_____

After you have answered the above questions, it is time to write a vision statement. Your goal is to create a vision everyone can see, feel and be inspired and excited by. Try phrasing your vision in terms of an image others can easily picture. (For example, "My dream is to create a vibrant community vegetable garden for my neighborhood." In contrast, a statement like "I want to make children happy" doesn't give other people enough context to understand your vision of how to make that happen.)

Once you have thought about it and written something, step away from it for a day or two. Then come back to re-write it. Make sure every word counts and cannot be misinterpreted, avoiding jargon or fancy words. You want everyone to know what your vision is, both at work and in your community. Your goal is to get your statement down to one succinct sentence.

Below are some organizations' vision statements that are effective and impactful using less than 15 words, which makes them easy to remember and repeat. This is what these companies envision for the world. They are simple and direct.

Feeding America: A hunger-free America (*3 words*)

National Multiple Sclerosis Society: A world free of MS (*5 words*)

Habitat for Humanity: A world where everyone has a decent place to live. (*10 words*)

Oceana: Seeks to make our oceans as rich, healthy and abundant as they once were. (*14 words*)

Now it's your turn. Make it visual and, if it's helpful, put it in context by saying "I envision a world in which _____."

"Company You" Vision Statement:

_____
_____
_____
_____
_____
_____

Your Mission Statement

Your mission statement communicates what you are going to do to achieve your vision. It is a concise statement that reflects the path you are taking to accomplish your vision. Your mission statement will keep you and your supporters on task and on the same page, moving forward together without drifting when business or strategic plans shift or the waters begin to get muddy.

Take a look at some of the action verbs below in some well-known organizational mission statements:

TED: Spreading ideas. (2 words)

The Humane Society: Celebrating animals, confronting cruelty. (4)

Wounded Warrior Project: To honor and empower wounded warriors. (6)

Ebay: Provide a global trading platform where practically anyone can trade practically anything. (12 words)

Feeding America: To feed America's hungry through a nationwide network of member food banks and engage our country in the fight to end hunger. (22 words)

These companies communicate a lot with their verbs! They're spreading, celebrating, confronting, honoring, empowering, providing, feeding and engaging. You know precisely and immediately how they plan to execute their vision.

Now it is your turn. Answer the questions below and then tackle writing your own mission statement. Write freely without worrying about the length and then come back to it again later to pare it down so anyone reading it knows what actions you will take each day.

1. List five actions to describe what you do, or will do, to make your work environment more fulfilling. For example, perhaps you will promote creativity, fun and innovation or support safety, education, growth opportunities, fair compensation and diversity.

_____

_____

_____

_____

_____

_____

_____

2. List five actions you do, or will do, for your community to make the world a better place. For example, solve a pressing social issue, share your work expertise, or serve certain markets who are receiving certain benefits.

_____

_____

_____

_____

_____

_____

_____

"Company You" Mission Statement:

Draft a succinct mission statement showing how you will achieve your vision through action.

_____

_____

_____

_____

_____

_____

Your Values Statement

Your values statement needs to incorporate a handful of your core values, many of which you have identified on this journey. It should be easily repeated, remembered and acted on, and must be in alignment with your mission and vision. It must also be visibly integrated into the way you show up in the world through your personal brand. Your values statement will attract others with the same values and same desire to leave a positive impact on the world.

What your values statement is not, is a code of ethics or platitudes used for marketing or hype or to fill up empty pages in a journal. It is a way of life and a framework you rely on as you make decisions.

When you are identifying your values for your values statement, start with action verbs. You can include more than one word as long as they are clear, concise and easy to memorize and apply. (For example, "Build to Last," "Share the Good," "Do the Right Thing," "Serve with Purpose," "Build the Team," "Do More with Less.")

Ask yourself:

1. What values do you already hold? What values do you wish were more evident in your life or to others? (Refer to your answers in Step One, if needed.)

_____

_____

_____

_____

_____

_____

_____

_____

_____

_____

2. What values are important to your stakeholders or those you impact (i.e., coworkers, community, family and friends, customers or clients)? How do you know this?

_____
_____
_____
_____
_____
_____
_____
_____

3. How are your values aligned with your vision and mission statements?

_____
_____
_____
_____
_____
_____
_____
_____

"Company You" Values Statement:

Write a values statement that is no-nonsense, active and unambiguous, showing the world through action verbs the boundaries within which you operate both at work and in your community.

_____
_____
_____
_____
_____
_____
_____

Remember to add your vision, mission and values statements to your clarity map before you move on to the next step. These are the guideposts you want to see daily and operate within.

Lesson Two:
Walking the Talk

You know what your values are, but how do you figure out the values of business entities or organizations of interest to you? First, it is important to realize that company values written on a website may not actually be representative of the core values at play. Some research will be needed to get a real sense of whether the values as written are an integral part of how the leaders manage the companies and the guideposts employees use when making decisions throughout their workdays. These principles and beliefs form the core of the culture and brand of the company.

There are many ways to find answers to your questions. Some resources that may be helpful include:

- Company career page
- LinkedIn company profile
- Facebook page
- Twitter profile
- Glassdoor (glassdoor.com)
- Yelp
- Google search (or any search engine)
- Job board postings
- Job board company description or page

- The Good Jobs (thegoodjobs.com)
- Current and former employees

In Lesson Two, you will look at the core values of at least three companies you are interested in or that may be interested in you. This exercise can be, and should be, repeated with any company you believe you resonate with to see how well you align. Your research should tell you the story of what life is like both within the organization and in its dealings with external stakeholders.

Answer the questions below to decide whether the candidate company is a good fit for you as an employer or other strategic business alliance. Include specific examples and where you found the information. Then, write the core value words you identified in Step One and those the company identifies with on the "Values Assessment" template at the end of this exercise to see how your pieces to the puzzle fit together.

As you know, each piece to a jigsaw puzzle is unique but, when fit together, they all contribute to make a completed picture.

Employees:

1. Are the employees "brand ambassadors" of the company, excited and proud to work there?

_____

_____

_____

_____

_____

_____

_____

_____

_____

_____

2. Are the employees engaged in the organization with a sense of ownership?

_____

_____

_____

_____

_____

_____

_____

3. Are the employees confident in the leadership?

_____

_____

_____

_____

_____

_____

_____

4. Are the employees proud of the company's products and services?

_____

_____

_____

_____

_____

_____

5. Is the employee base diversified and is there pay equality?

_____

_____

_____

_____

_____

_____

6. What did the employees say the company core value words are?

_____

_____

_____

_____

_____

_____

_____

_____

Management:

1. Are the leaders of the company role models for the employees and other stakeholders?

_____

_____

_____

_____

_____

_____

_____

_____

2. Does the company have a mentoring program or offer training programs?

_____

_____

_____

_____

_____

_____

_____

_____

_____

_____

3. Does the management team talk about particular success stories of their employees?

_____

_____

_____

_____

_____

_____

4. How are core values communicated and enforced throughout the company?

_____

_____

_____

_____

_____

_____

5. Do the leaders provide a culture of innovation?

_____

_____

_____

_____

_____

_____

6. What did management say the company core value words are?

_____

_____

_____

_____

_____

_____

Other stakeholders (i.e., consumers, vendors, investors):

1. Do the products and services score well in terms of quality?

   _____

   _____

   _____

   _____

   _____

   _____

   _____

   _____

2. Does the company offer a high degree of customer care through its employees?

   _____

   _____

   _____

   _____

   _____

   _____

3. Are vendors paid in a timely manner and are their relationships with the company managed with integrity?

   _____

   _____

   _____

   _____

   _____

   _____

   _____

   _____

4. Are investors interested in the sustainability of the business as well as the rate of return?

_____
_____
_____
_____
_____
_____
_____
_____
_____

5. Are the customers and other stakeholders brand ambassadors?

_____
_____
_____
_____
_____
_____
_____
_____
_____

6. What did the stakeholders say the company core value words are?

_____
_____
_____
_____
_____
_____
_____
_____
_____

Community:

1. Does the company partner with nonprofits in their local community in ways other than cash donations?

   _____
   _____
   _____
   _____
   _____
   _____
   _____
   _____

2. Does the company have programs enabling employees to "give back?"

   _____
   _____
   _____
   _____
   _____
   _____
   _____
   _____

3. Is the company environmentally conscious and how does it reduce any negative footprint?

   _____
   _____
   _____
   _____
   _____
   _____
   _____

4. Does the company have an internship program?

_____
_____
_____
_____
_____
_____
_____

5. Does the company have a solid compliance program?

_____
_____
_____
_____
_____
_____
_____

6. What does the community say the company core value words are?

_____
_____
_____
_____
_____
_____
_____

These questions are just the beginning of your research. Your next step is to take the information you have accumulated and find the commonalities and differences between your values and those of the organizations you are considering aligning with so you can make an informed decision. I have included a template to help you make that comparison or you can download a copy of it at solutionariesacademy.com/templates if you'd prefer.

With over half of our current workforce (including both the unemployed as well as employed) looking for work that fulfills them, we know a value match increases the odds of success in terms of both emotional fulfillment and continued growth within the organization. Fortunately, the world of business is beginning to wake up to the sobering fact that if they don't provide a value exchange with their workforce, they will face a decisive talent gap in the upcoming years. This is your time to have a voice regarding the things that mean the most to you.

Values Assessment

Organization: _____

My Values	Where Values Align	Company Values

Lesson Three:
Your Value Train

We have talked about the value exchange between Company You and other organizations. Even if you are not looking for a new job or opportunity today, I'm confident you would like to strengthen the exchange and recognition of value at your own company or organizations you are involved with.

In this step, you will look at how you, as a Solutionary, can bring your values to work to create an environment that fulfills your emotional needs.

Being part of a values-based and socially responsible organization is not confined to the "four walls" of the company. Rather, it extends to all stakeholders, internal and external, and shows up in the exchanges between all parties. If this continual exchange of value is in balance, it reflects well on your business. It results in you being perceived as a solid global citizen and respected corporate partner who is here for the long term and who cares about the issues facing our world today.

Your Stakeholders

Who are the people or groups with the power to respond to, negotiate with and change the strategic future of your company? They are the stakeholders, the passengers on your Value Train.

Your community is reflected in:

- The **consumers** who purchase products and have a need fulfilled.
- The **investors** who believe in the company's efforts and dedicate time and money so it can achieve its goals and thereby share in the rewards.
- The **employees** who offer their skills and expertise in exchange for financial remuneration and personal fulfillment.
- The **neighborhoods** around your place of business and anyone whose daily existence is changed because of the actions or presence of your company.

Your company's impact to the planet is reflected by its concern for its carbon footprint and use of natural resources. Compliance programs care about the sustainability of the company and their investors' financial support. Dedicated social responsibility programs reflect a concern for their people, profit and planet.

Stakeholders can be internal or external, junior or senior, and positive or negative influencers. The one thing they have in common is that they impact the organization in some way or it impacts them. Because there are literally hundreds of potential stakeholders for every company, it is best to prioritize them and determine the importance of their relationships.

Make an exhaustive list of your company's stakeholders and then go through it and sort them. Remember, negative impact can be as relevant as positive impact where the business is concerned. You might categorize them by internal/external, positive/negative impact, department/job titles, vendor types, environmental/community impact, etc. To help you out, I have provided a list of potential stakeholders in a Stakeholder Master List at solutionariesacademy.com/bonuses.

After you have made a list of stakeholders and sorted them, you will want to analyze the value (or impact) your company receives from them and the value (or impact) they receive from your company.

Finally, put some thought into ways your company can significantly improve that value exchange. Write down one action item for each category below that your company can take and, more specifically, how you can support that effort.

- Consumers: _____
- Investors: _____
- Employees: _____
- Community: _____
- Environment: _____

Your Employer Brand

While you are trying to define the value exchange between your company and your stakeholders, it is helpful to understand how your company's culture is reflected to the world around it and to those very stakeholders, in particular to potential employees.

Different from a commercial product brand, an employer brand is sometimes called a "culture brand." It reflects the values of your company, the work environment and the people who believe in it and support it.

To some extent, it is a collective of the personal brands of each of the employees and the imprint they leave behind with every contact they make. Ultimately, it represents your company's reputation as an employer and the employment experience people can expect to have at your company.

Remember, recruits investigate companies starting with Google searches and reviews, checking out their presence on social media, and asking their friends and family for input about their own experiences with your company or product. Informal employer branding already exists whether you attempt to shape it or not due to the impression your employees leave behind on others working with the company.

This is not unlike your personal brand that you investigated back in Step Two. In this case, your company needs to stand out as an innovative leader, one that is in it for the long haul and cares about its employees, communities and investors.

Developing an employer brand takes time and careful thought. In this step, you will identify what the brand is today in terms of the value your company offers to its talent. This will become the baseline. With this information, you can begin to strategize how to create the employer brand you would like to have and adjustments you might need to make.

Take a few minutes to answer the following questions:

1. What attributes do recruits and employees identify with your company? Are they aligned with the company's core values as listed? Are they broader including things like high tech or a fun work environment?

_____

_____

_____

_____

_____

_____

_____

_____

_____

_____

_____

_____

_____

_____

_____

2. Does your company have an employee profile to help understand the types of employees that thrive best in the company (for example, men, women, Millennials, Boomers, etc.)? Are you aware of typical characteristics of current employees—those that work best and those that don't? Describe.

_____

_____

_____

_____

_____

_____

_____

3. Does your company run focus groups and survey current employees to compare the differences between their experiences and views of the organization and the ideal attributes it wants the employer brand to reflect?

_____

_____

_____

_____

_____

_____

_____

4. Does the organization find ways to close the gap between words and actions to create more engaged employees and brand advocates?

_____

_____

_____

_____

_____

_____

_____

5. Does the business closely examine its competitors' recruiting and hiring practices, company culture and employee perks? How can it distinguish what it has to offer from its competitors?

    _____

    _____

    _____

    _____

    _____

    _____

    _____

6. What promises does your business make to current and future employees about its corporate culture and what they can expect as a valued member?

    _____

    _____

    _____

    _____

    _____

    _____

    _____

7. Does your company have a communication strategy for all the actions and messages a potential employee receives from the organization? Are candidate viewpoints supported by the reality of the workplace? How are current perceptions affecting your ability to recruit top talent?

    _____

    _____

    _____

    _____

    _____

    _____

    _____

8. Does the business externally show its employer brand through the company website, social media, job ads, career fairs and other events? Does it use video to show rather than tell? Does it update profiles frequently? Does it concentrate on sharing the culture rather than selling it? Explain.

_____

_____

_____

_____

_____

_____

9. Does it track and engage with comments about the company on sites like Twitter, Facebook and Glassdoor to gauge how effective the employer brand is?

_____

_____

_____

_____

_____

_____

10. Does it conduct exit interviews? What do exit interviews reveal about the reasons and number of employees that have left within six months to one year of employment? What has the financial cost been to the company?

_____

_____

_____

_____

_____

_____

Just as you learned to attract your tribe of kindred spirits through your personal brand, it is equally as important for companies soliciting new employees to show they appreciate their contributions. Values attract values. Are there ways you can participate in growing this value exchange at your company? If you are building a new company of your own, will you embed these values into its core foundation and start your social responsibility programs from its inception?

Ways to participate in social impact are varied! You can find a like-minded business, create one of your own, or support and enhance the value exchange at your current company. Every path leads to greater joy on the job.

Step Six

Each Step You Take

*Solutionaries leave a blueprint
for future generations
to continue the path of innovation.*

Your Journey, Your Legacy

When you began this journey just a short time ago, you were looking for "something." Perhaps, your career felt stalled or boring or the daily news left you feeling overwhelmed with a desire to make a change. Whether you are a new graduate or a stay-at-home mother returning to the workforce or a corporate executive thinking about your legacy, the reasons we decide to take stock of ourselves, our work and our values are varied. The common thread, however, is that we all want to have more fulfilling lives and a more positive impact on the world.

As you have worked your way through this book, you have:

- Clarified and owned your core values by studying life experiences that left an impact on you.

- Assessed how you present yourself to the world and found ways you can better define and manage that perception.

- Identified issues and causes that inspire or bother you and agreed to commit time and energy to the ones that particularly resonate with you.

- Defined your tribe, kindred spirits with the same goals and dreams, and identified ways you can reach them and ways they can find you.

- Analyzed your value proposition and matched it with companies, organizations and causes that will benefit from it even as your emotional reservoir is filled.

- Discovered a gap in the marketplace that needs servicing so a pressing social issue can be addressed.

Now it is time to create a strategy and plan for a life that includes work with meaning as well as a paycheck. I don't know anyone who wouldn't like to have work that both fulfills them and supports them!

It can be daunting to find ourselves considering, or in the midst of, transition. So, in this section, you will come up with a plan you can actually execute.

In this discovery process, you have identified companies in industry sectors you find exciting and inspiring, and ways you can align with them. Whether it's through employment, volunteer work or by creating a social enterprise, you are now ready to outline how you will become involved.

In Lesson One, you will begin to create the framework for a basic business plan for Company You and how you plan to achieve your goals.

In Lesson Two, I have provided a basic checklist for the initial steps required to create a social enterprise, if that's the path you choose to follow.

And finally, in Lesson Three, you will make a commitment to yourself and the world to keep moving forward on this journey that will offer you amazing new friends and coworkers, adventures, opportunities and rewards. Once on the road, you will never look back.

Lesson One: Plan the Trip

In Step Six, you are going to drive your "stake in the sand" and develop a plan of attack—the steps you can take in the coming months to actualize your vision. This is your opportunity to put pen to paper and create a detailed outline.

It might also be a perfect time for you to review the vision, mission and values statements you created in Step Five. Remember, your mission statement is a macro-view of your path forward. Now it's time to create the micro-view, a comprehensive step-by-step plan.

"Company You" Business Plan

Every solid business has a business plan outlining how it will reach its goals. It is a living document because it is not just written and then tucked away in a file. Rather, it becomes a blueprint that acts as a reference and framework when unanticipated events occur or the path becomes murky. No one wants an eclectic business left to chance or constant deviations. A business plan will keep the team on course.

The business plan for "Company You" is no different than that of a well-run organization. You should have a quarterly plan for at least twelve months out. For some, it is also helpful and fun to give each quarter a theme as it breaks the plan into targeted project groups. For example, one quarter's theme might be "Online Presence" with the focus on how you show up in social media, on your website or in blogs.

Another quarter might be "Engaging My Tribe" where the focus is on finding networking groups, companies or individuals with common interests, and ways you will contact them and establish a relationship.

Although there are many sophisticated project plans and mind-mapping websites, they can be a little intimidating for those not technologically savvy. The truth is, you began to frame your "Company You" plan with the clarity map you created in Step Three and have continued to fill in throughout this process.

Take the items you have identified on that map and move them to a spreadsheet or project planning program and, under each one, write every single step that needs to happen to accomplish the task. Your plan must have target dates and completion dates for each item on it. This reflects a commitment by you to get them done on time.

Accountability Partners

It is easy to make excuses about not reaching self-imposed goals, but I think we all know if we don't have them… nothing gets done. I find having an accountability partner can be a great help. This can be a friend or colleague you like and respect or a person you can trust to keep you honest and moving forward on the plan you have created. Find someone who encourages you to proceed down the path rather than condemning you if you don't—or it won't be an inspirational situation, one aligned with success. You want someone who will be your cheerleader, help you see the light at the end of the tunnel when things seem dark, and celebrate your victories.

In addition, an accountability partner can help you identify weaknesses in your business or professional goals and help you make plans to overcome them. But it is not their job to change your life. It is up to you to tell them what your goals are and provide weekly updates including the willingness to own your own mistakes, such as a failure to meet a deadline. The relationship will be even more motivating if there are rewards and consequences if you reach or fail to meet a desired outcome you set at the beginning. It can be as simple as a dinner out or a gift card for a certain amount.

Below, list names of potential accountability partners who might be a good fit for you, why you think they are a good fit for you, and what you have to offer them:

1. _____
   _____
   _____
   _____
   _____

2. _____
   _____
   _____
   _____
   _____

3. _____
   _____
   _____
   _____
   _____

Now, plan to contact each of them this week to see if they will meet with you to discuss a working or mentoring relationship, whether formal or informal. Before your meeting, outline your desires and expectations so that you will be able to clearly articulate your needs. It is important that that you be able to discuss how you expect this process to unfold in terms of schedules and time commitments.

Remember, the word *partner* implies that you will be contributing something to this relationship. What does the other person need? How can you help them?

Masterminds

Critical to the success of any partnering relationship is having preset times and locations to meet. Committing to reach certain goals within a specified period of time is what will keep you progressing and seeing results. This can be a little tougher with two people's schedules, which is why making the commitment to a group of people, as in a mastermind, is a better fit for many. It offers the opportunity to share your own wisdom while you give back to others with the same desire to fulfill their dreams—one of the primary reasons you began this journey.

The beauty of belonging to a mastermind is that there is a structure. You have a group of business advisers and your network is expanded exponentially and rapidly. That feeling of being alone as you pursue your vision is reduced when you are part of a group of supporters you meet with on a consistent basis. Other peoples' skills and experiences are unique and may offer you a wealth of information. Often, members work together on projects and cross-promote each other even as they form lifelong friendships built on mutual respect.

Below, list options for mastermind groups that might be a good fit for you:

1. _____

2. _____

3. _____

As a huge advocate for masterminds, I would like to extend an invitation to you to become part of my mastermind group. Through my Solutionaries Academy, I offer three different types of support that will help you at any stage of your journey. You can find out more at solutionariesacademy.com.

If you find yourself thinking as you read this book that you would enjoy having my encouragement and a team approach as you navigate through the exercises, please join our group of changemakers and let's do this together! You are exercising muscles you may not have used for a long time and going through the process with others may be just the inspiration you need while offering you a whole new set of viewpoints. Plus, I provide an online library with additional materials, community calls and personal one on one coaching to help you get exactly where you want to go. Seats are limited for each class to make it a personal experience. Save yours at solutionariesacademy.com/illuminate.

Metrics

Along the way you need to measure and evaluate your progress to determine if you are on the right track and if you are making headway executing your plan. Look at the challenges and victories you have had and decide if you need to adjust your course of action. This includes taking stock of the resources or tools you will need to advance. Remember, it is all about making your plan and then working it.

I have also included a sample annual planner to kick-start writing your plan for the year. You can start it at any time of the year and the topics or themes for the months can be changed or moved. To begin, try filling in this one to give you a solid understanding of how creating a basic framework will help you nail down your goals. (Feel free to download a copy from solutionariesacademy.com/templates.)

It's time to step out with conviction!

Annual Planner

JANUARY	FEBRUARY	MARCH
Polish My Physical Presence	Hone My Expertise	Expand My Business Network

APRIL	MAY	JUNE
Engage with My Community	Align with My Tribe	Show My Expertise

JULY	AUGUST	SEPTEMBER
Improve My Resume & Bio	Create My Brand Identity	Sharpen My Presentation Skills

OCTOBER	NOVEMBER	DECEMBER
Refine My Social Media Presence	Step Up My Leadership Roles	Participate in Innovation

Lesson Two:
Your Unique Solution

Somewhere along the way, you may have decided you would like to venture out on your own and create a business to address a socially pressing issue and make a healthy return while doing so. Perhaps the impetus was that you discovered no one is focused on the issue in the way you believe it needs to be managed or that there is room in the market for other players to make a real impact.

Welcome to the world of social enterprise, a hybrid business with characteristics of both for profit and not-for-profit businesses.

Social enterprises are businesses that provide innovative solutions to problems affecting large quantities of people or our planet. The world of nonprofits, previously anointed the caretakers and problem-solvers of all social issues, cannot keep up with the demand for solutions. Enter the world of businesses stepping forward to provide funds and expertise so solutions can be scaled at a rate greater than problems can increase.

These hybrid businesses have a social mission as well as a mandate to show a solid return on investment to their shareholders. It's not always easy to achieve the perfect balance between social responsibility and a healthy bottom line.

When I think of the life of a social entrepreneur, I am reminded of a gymnast at the Olympics carefully navigating the balance beam, a 10-centimeter wide wood beam requiring maximum dexterity and steadiness. The athlete does flips, turns and dismounts using every bit of her skills not to fall off the beam.

For the social entrepreneur, one side of the beam is the world of nonprofits, built on passion and the desire to help those less fortunate or the underdog cause. These organizations are often viewed skeptically by the public as incapable of strategic business management. To the other side is the myopic world of big business focused on bottom-line profits and maximum returns to shareholders to the exclusion of all else. These businesses and shareholders are often viewed by the market as greedy.

The trick is to remember that the vision of a social purpose business is to create a shift, a change that deeply affects the lives of many, not just solving individual problems like a company does through product sales. The mission is to get there in a responsible, accountable and sustainable way. The values are those you choose to operate within as you present your business to the world.

As the leader, you will need to stay strong and focused, with a view of the greater picture even when many will demand attention for their own agendas. In other words, you will need to consistently connect to the heart of the work even as you run your company like a profitable business. After all, without a solid rate of return, there are no funds to solve the problem you hope eradicate.

In Lesson Two, you will begin outlining the framework for your new venture so you can do just that.

Let's start with what is motivating you to consider a social enterprise and explore the stories of the people or cause you would like to support. Below, connect to the cause personally by writing and sharing some of these stories. They will act as your guideposts, helping you stay focused as you forge ahead.

This is not unlike the work you did in Step One when you described people who have made an impact on you and in Step Three when you identified causes and described why they are important to you.

Now, your assignment is to describe three different situations, the people involved, their stories and why they touched you. Take time to explain how the outcome would have been different if your solution had been available and offered to them. Be detailed and create a visual for all of us so we can see and understand the importance. This is your heart line or emotional connection to your new venture.

1. _____
   _____
   _____
   _____
   _____
   _____
   _____
   _____

2. _____
   _____
   _____
   _____
   _____
   _____
   _____
   _____

3. _____
   _____
   _____
   _____
   _____
   _____
   _____
   _____

Social Enterprise Checklist

Even though a social enterprise has a vision to solve a socially pressing issue, it must still be run like any other profitable business. It must have a clear strategy with a goal to make a healthy return for its investors even as it marches toward its vision. Because your business plan is for a social enterprise, you will continually tie in what sets you apart in terms of your commitment to social innovation.

As you begin to put your plan together, you will need to respond fully to each of the topics in the list below. Your responses will help you create a clear understanding of the business aspects of the company before you spend a lot of money launching it.

Remember, just one bite of the elephant at a time! This is not an extended business plan but an important first step allowing you to articulate your vision and explain how you will make it happen.

1. **Executive Summary:** Give a high-level description of your company, its vision, the issue it will resolve and how it will solve it.

2. **Team:** Identify your team and provide their bios as well as what they bring to the organization.

3. **Market Landscape:** Describe your competitors, if any, or other stakeholders in the space, their successes and challenges, as well as their products and services.

4. **Product or Service Distinction:** Describe what sets your company/product apart and makes it unique. This is a perfect time to talk about its social impact.

5. **Customers or Clients:** Describe exactly who is interested in your product and why, what they will receive, and how it will impact them or solve a problem for them.

6. **Marketing Strategy:** Describe the ways you will tell the world about your new venture and engage customers or clients. This is another great time to tie in your social innovation efforts.

7. **Business Structure:** Outline your organization's business structure. As a social purpose business, you may be interested in forming a benefit corporation or receiving certification as a B Corp.

8. **Barriers to Entry:** Talk about the hurdles you will need to cross to be successful in your venture and some ways you will do this. Be sure to research others' efforts to do the same.

9. **Pricing Model:** Detail your pricing and how you have arrived at these numbers.

10. **Financial Model:** Describe how the business will be funded and the revenue/expense model. (You will be putting together projections to complete this section if you don't have them already.) How are you going to make a profit to fund your heart work?

All business plans seem a little intimidating if you look at them as a whole. After all, it's a lot of information to acquire and process! But I have confidence in you. The only advice I can give you is to sit down at your computer and just dig in, one baby step at a time. Keep your vision, mission and values in front of you at all times as a reminder of your dreams and look at your clarity map daily. It will help if, and when, you get caught in the weeds. But don't worry about it. We all do!

Lesson Three:
Commit to Yourself

As you come to the end of this journey, you may face your toughest challenge yet, staying true to yourself and true to your dreams and desires. Human beings by their very nature are driven by tasks and goals. The end of each race represents a sense of accomplishment. We are proud that the thing we aspired to do has been mastered.

The tough part is when we create goals that are unreachable or goals we can't really relate to—ones our head tells us we should aim for, but our heart isn't into. Those are often the items we record on our New Year's list, pin to the refrigerator and forget. If you don't create an action plan to make them happen and you haven't really identified why they are deeply important to you, everyday life will take over and these little dreams often take a backseat.

In Step Three, you began work on your clarity map. This creative exercise and tool should now reflect:

- Your values. (*Step One*)

- Ways you will show up in the world as a reflection of those values. (*Step Two*)

- Two to three issues that interest you or bother you. (*Step Three*)

- Your tribe of individuals or organizations that are working to address those very issues and ways you will engage with them. (*Step Four*)

- How your values line up with your tribe and ways you will be able to contribute. (*Step Five*)

By the end of Step Six, you will add the actions to your clarity map that you are committed to take in the coming months to create a lasting, positive impact at your place of work and in your community.

One of the reasons for asking you to *commit* to yourself and the world rather than making a *promise* to yourself is that the two words have a subtle, but important, difference. When you make a commitment, you add the factor of trust, as opposed to a promise, which is action-driven only.

You have spent your time well: reading this book, digging deep, searching for the values and issues meaningful to you, as well as the places and ways you can contribute. These priceless values make you unique and special. They deserve a heartfelt commitment that you will follow through with your desire to make a difference.

So how do you get out of the "do-er" mode into a "heart-connected" mode? The first step is to go back to the very reasons you were drawn to the issues that touched you and drew you to them (Step Three). You were asked to relate personal experiences and stories that attracted you to the topic or organization. Let's take it one step farther.

In the section below, write the issue that you would like to focus your time and energy on and then underneath write how this issue makes you feel when you hear or read about it. The feelings may range from sadness or frustration, if it is something that bothers you, to excitement and hope, if it is a topic that inspires you.

In the second part of the exercise, you will be asked to come up with words to describe the feelings you would experience if you were part of the solution or change, or if you could create a positive impact because of your engagement with the project.

Find a quiet place to get in touch with your feelings. Think about the life experience you had that drew you to the project and how you felt when you had that experience as well as whether it continues to impact you. Finally, consider your deepest desire and hope for it. Then, start writing.

Topic One: _____

When I hear or read about this issue it makes me feel:

_____
_____
_____
_____
_____
_____
_____

If I could help, I would feel: _____

_____
_____
_____
_____
_____
_____
_____

Topic Two: _____

When I hear or read about this issue it makes me feel:

_____
_____
_____
_____
_____
_____
_____

If I could help, I would feel: _____

_____

_____

_____

_____

_____

_____

_____

_____

Topic Three:_____

When I hear or read about this issue it makes me feel:

_____

_____

_____

_____

_____

_____

_____

If I could help, I would feel: _____

_____

_____

_____

_____

_____

_____

_____

Ultimately, the most important words you will add to your clarity map will be those that engage your commitment. There will be days when it is hard to hold the vision—where you might be short on cheerleaders and the only one you see is in the mirror. Your map will inspire and reengage you, while acting as a reminder of the values and the things you hold dear. It will prompt you to participate, even if you think you don't have time and can't see the way.

The world needs you to light the path. After all, if not you, then who? And if not now, then when?

Thank you for reading *Solutionaries*. If you've enjoyed this book, please leave a review on Amazon, Goodreads or your favorite review site. It helps me reach more people so they too can find ways to do well while doing good.

As you start to explore your own unique way of solving the issues that have meaning to you, you may find yourself wanting to be part of community of other solutionaries. Should that be the case, I encourage you to take a look at my Solutionaires Academy at solutionariesacademy.com. There you will find different types of masterminds, online classes and workshops that will help you on any leg of your journey.

Note from the Author

A dream or reality... Which will it be for you? All great accomplishments, inventions, movements or trends start with a spark of inspiration. As sure as the waves roll onto the shore one after the other, or the comforting knowledge that night will follow the day, each of us will have millions of thoughts every waking hour. As a special bonus, some of us will receive gifts of information in the middle of the night that can seem watered down and lackluster in the practical light of day, but should not be discarded. I invite you to spend a little time thinking about those dreams. Your subconscious is reminding you of the things that are important to you.

Many have convinced themselves that their dreams to do something "important" are just beyond their fingertips, not quite reachable, certainly not practical. Have you ever said with a sigh, "I woke up from my dream to reality"? If your answer is "yes," consider that you gave life to this thought rather than taking action to make your dream your reality. Dreams are actually realized, my friends. They just need a little energy behind them—they need you to do something about the dream. They are asking you to take the time to acknowledge them and breathe some life into them.

Every day, companies step up and into the world of social responsibility, understanding that only the business acumen of their talent-base and deep pockets will turn the tide of issues our world faces. Nonprofits, previously anointed with responsibility for handling all social issues, are learning how to run their organizations more efficiently, making better use of their resources. The government sector is passing legislation state-by-state, country-by-country, providing vehicles for social purpose companies to succeed. Solutionaries, people just like you and me, without a lot of money or backing, are also stepping forward and making a difference.

I want to thank you for allowing me to act as your guide, to considering new possibilities, to being receptive to different viewpoints and to challenging discussions. Social innovators and those hopeful for a better world, think and dream in a very big way. They see the world as manageable. They see the possibilities for transformation and they, like you, are driven by a passion to help. They understand that every action we take in business affects the entire ecosystem of our community and our world.

You are at the forefront and in good company with many others who know there is a more thoughtful and inclusive way to leave a positive impact and an admirable legacy for our children and their children.

Congratulations for all the value you bring to this world. Our puzzle cannot be solved without the piece you hold.

Linda

Acknowledgments

When I look back at my life's journey, so many people and experiences have shaped me to be the woman that I am today. I was fortunate to have been born to parents, Bill and Betty Lattimore, who loved me unconditionally. From the moment I arrived, I was encouraged to be and do anything that brought me joy and they reminded me that I also was responsible to my family, friends and extended community. I was accountable for my actions and... inactions. They set my moral compass.

My sister, Dr. Carol Lattimore, continues to support me every day, encouraging me when I fall down and laughing with me when it seems to be the only recourse. As a college English professor, she was the perfect first editor for Solutionaries. She made sure that my words accurately portrayed my intention even though there were times I wanted to throttle her needling, like all sisters are prone to do.

My precious daughters, Allie Lindenmuth and Rachel Kiner, have been glued to my hip and heart from the day they were born, perhaps even more so as I faced single motherhood for many years. They continue to say, "I'm proud of you, Mom. You can do this!" And, that is all a mother could ever ask for. In many respects, they are my North Star.

This book would have never manifested as quickly as it did without the efforts of my third "daughter," Tegan Bitner, who has steadfastly stood by me as my right hand for the last seven years. She is as much a part of my family as if she were my biological daughter and I owe her a debt of gratitude for her constant faith in me and this work.

Tara Alemany and Mark Gerber from Emerald Lake Books were referred to me by another happy author. I appreciate their patience and thoughtfulness in guiding a newbie (in terms of publishing a book) through the process. This has been a collaborative team effort and I look forward to more books and years of publishing together.

After I left law school, I was fortunate to have wonderful mentors during my career that gave me the tools to be a good mentor myself. I want to thank Judge Mary Bacon (deceased), Jim Powers, Colleen Anderson, Bob Craig, Dr. Sara Gilman, Sister Dorothy Ettling (deceased), Dr. Mohammad Yunus, Jane Deuber and Les Brown, just to name a few. I know with certainty that everyone that crosses my path is, in fact, a mentor and someone who I can learn from.

My dear friend, Barbara Strobel, has walked by my side since I was 24 years old. Her unwavering love and support has seen me through good times and tough times from the birth of my babies to marriage troubles to the loss of my parents. She has been my cheerleader from one business idea to the next, giving me practical advice as a CPA and hope and faith when things seem impossible.

Sandie Marrinucci has unselfishly offered her brilliance on many occasions when I have found myself stuck for just the right words for my latest blog or catchy title for a book chapter. Her skills as a writer are unparalleled and her loving friendship is one I will cherish forever.

Every woman needs a "girl squad," the recipients of exhausted late-night phone calls, celebrants of victories, bootstrappers after falls, and pullies when we get stuck. A big thank you to my forever peeps: Vanessa Gilmore, Carla Powers, Ann Friedman, Pamela Merritt, Rosa Glenn Reilly, Nancy Brennan, Pat Kellough, Stacey Canfield, Susan Gibson,

Kimber Kabell, Cherie Matthews, Eileen Padberg, Felena Hanson, Sue Snyder, Shirleen Renee Davies, Tonya Johannsen, Francesca San Diego and Luisa Piette. There are so many more amazing men and women that have been a part of my life and I'm proud to say that we continue to hold high the torch of peace and collaboration and hope for a better world.

It takes a village and mine is robust and connected. I'm deeply thankful for all who cross my path each day offering me words of wisdom, lessons and texture to a life I believe is well lived!

About the Author

Linda Lattimore is a dedicated and passionate collaborator and visionary. She is the Founder and Executive Director of the WGN Global Fund (wgn-globalfund.org), a 501c(3) that teaches young leaders about social enterprise as a vehicle for change and gives them the tools  to act as role models for future generations. In addition, WGF supports the Global Business Partners program, which joins forces with women in developing nations who, because of socio-economic circumstances, would not otherwise have access to the education or funding opportunities needed to create small businesses.

Linda is a well-regarded speaker, published author and educator in the field of Sustained Leadership (lindalattimore.com). As the Founder of Cross Sector Institute (xsectorinstitute.com), she is committed to business models that recognize the significance of social responsibility. Her emphasis is on encouraging clients to create thriving corporate responsibility programs and to do good even as they do well.

A seasoned lawyer, C-suite executive and business strategist, she is committed to helping individuals, from Millennials to Boomers, understand the importance of their unique gifts and talents to a world in need. An American raised in Latin America, she has traveled extensively throughout the world as international corporate counsel, witnessing first-hand some of the world's most pressing social issues.

Linda is the proud mother of two outstanding young women who carry the torch of service and community give-back that generations before them held high.

Visit us at
emeraldlakebooks.com

CPSIA information can be obtained
at www.ICGtesting.com
Printed in the USA
LVHW05s1546030518
575854LV00031B/1002/P